THE RAGING WAR OF IDEAS

How to Take Back our Faith, Family, and Country

By

Jason Jimenez

CONTENTS

To my precious children:
Tyler, Amy, Jackson, and Hailey.

May your lives be enriched by Christ, and
your futures filled with the gift of freedom!

You are my joy and crown!

FOREWORD

〜

By Dr. Norman L. Geisler

For the past 60 years God has privileged me to train young people to engage our changing times with God's unchanging truth. As a result, literally hundreds of young men and women are scattered around our country and around the world proclaiming God's absolute commands to our relativistic culture.

Few students among them are more anchored to the Rock and geared to the times than Jason Jimenez. Few have combined a more solid knowledge of God's Word with a thorough understanding of the culture and a passion to reach our milieu with God's message than the author of *The Raging War of Ideas*. This powerful and helpful book offers practical insight into the social upheavals (such as: cultural relativism, homosexuality, and the Islamic Revolution) which threaten our Christian faith, demoralize our families, and attempt to thwart the freedoms we are privileged to possess as Americans!

As a result of the pervasive influence of a postmodern culture, the right to life, traditional marriage, and the very foundations of the Christian Church are under heavy attack. If you are ready to have your eyes opened and your life challenged, read this book! In it, Jason Jimenez brings together years of biblical and apologetic training and experience as a pastor to set forth for the reader a compelling argument why all of us should be engaged in this culture and stand up as individuals, families, and as a Church to defend and live out the gospel of Jesus Christ.

The Raging War of Ideas is a must read for any Christian who desires to develop a biblical worldview, safeguard their homes, and jump start a campaign to literally transform their country from the inside out. You will not be the same after reading this book!

INTRODUCTION

$\smile$

At this very moment in time, there is an intense war over who will control the future destiny of our faith, families and country in America. A war that goes much deeper than opinion or political expediency. It's a war that rages over ideas.

Each of us possesses our own set of ideas that fundamentally define and shape us as humans. But how do we measure whose ideas are right and wrong? Whose ideas will rule and whose ideas will be obliterated and sink into obscurity?

This raging war of ideas goes beyond simple differences of opinion. *It is a cosmic battle between two diametrically opposed worldviews.* On the one hand: a worldview based on a Judeo-Christian ethic that believes in absolute truth, standards for moral living and religious freedom—which will be referred to as *traditionalism*. On the other: a worldview that denies the existence of objective truth and moral absolutes—which we define as *cultural relativism*.

In this book, you will come face-to-face with cultural relativism and its threefold effect that seeks to remove God, redefine truth, and replace Christianity. Because proponents of cultural relativism want to forcibly legislate this viewpoint on others, you will also learn to recognize their agenda and tactics and ways to defeat it. If these major threats—removing God, redefining truth, and replacing Christianity—go unchallenged, they will tear down the traditional framework erected by our Founders. The consequences will be catastrophic.

This nation was founded on the ideas and principles of freedom, liberty, and "In God We Trust." America was not founded on a pluralistic framework (i.e. belief that all opposing views are equally true). Our Founders believed in one Creator God who established absolute truth and therefore ordained standards of morality, ethics and values to live by. America's forefathers sacrificed their lives for the future hope of peace, freedom and prosperity in a Republic that would champion these great ideals.

Over the better part of the last century, however, America has been exchanging the written truths of our Founders for a new world order. One that opposes the very principles this nation was founded upon. With increasing regularity we witness our free market being replaced with a socialist one. We read rewritten versions of American history in textbooks throughout our schools. We see the U.S. Constitution revised with idealism. And most strikingly, we see our Judeo-Christian ethics swept away for situational ethics.

What has happened to the values of Samuel Adams? John Hancock? Patrick Henry? George Washington? Abraham Lincoln? What would they say if they were here to witness the circumstances America finds itself in today? Have the sacrifices for freedom been squandered?

More than ever, America is desperate for leaders who will offer real solutions that will turn our country around. Our country needs wise and charitable leaders who will lead with moral conviction and bring a halt to our current slide into ruination. It is incumbent upon us to pray daily for leaders who will take back the reigns of this country and help us regain a place of respect and trust once more.

Families all across this great land must wake up to the impending threats that seek to destroy our faith, families, and country. In my years working with families, I have witnessed how ignorant and disengaged the church and generations of families have become in our culture. Many evangelical Americans are frustrated and concerned about what is happening, but are unsure how to make a difference or become part of the solution.

If we are not equipped and active with regard to the cultural issues and policies of our day, we will essentially give up our freedoms to those who will legislate their *own* morality and govern how we live our lives. Ironically, it was from this same type of tyranny that our Founders and their families fled in search of a new life; a life of freedom and hope; a life which they found on the shores of North America. We must not fail to recognize today's threats to our freedom and allow ignorance or apathy to usher in an era of modern-day tyranny.

Although the beacon of hope and opportunity that America once offered has grown dim, there is still a window of opportunity to reignite our country's fervor to bring peace and stability to the world. America hangs in a veritable balance as it decides whether it will look to God and His principles or turn away. If America does abandon its dependence on Christianity, then the future of this country will undoubtedly grow dark.

It is my prayer that this book awakens Christians in America and sparks a resurgence to take back our faith, families and country. This is a grassroots effort to urge all Christians to return to the God-given precepts this nation was founded on and use them to reach the next generation with the gospel. It is foundational that people evaluate their beliefs and be proactive in transforming their lives and their families, thereby impacting the country for the greater good.

We must take a stand. We must pray that God gives us the strength and courage to fight this raging war of ideas. We must not abandon the call to challenge and engage our culture with unwavering truth and rise up as a new generation, inspired to live free and moral lives unto God. The future of our Christian faith and prosperity of our families depends upon us.

Jason Jimenez
Fall 2012
Charlotte, NC

PART ONE

The War to Destroy Our Faith

CHAPTER 1

Our Christian Heritage

"Having undertaken, for the glory of God, and advancement of the Christian faith, and honour of our king and country, a voyage to plant the first colony in the Northerne parts of Virginia..."[1] Mayflower Compact

The backbone of our great nation starts and ends with our Christian heritage. This bedrock was securely built with the morals and convictions of those brave settlers that first set foot on American soil. The Mayflower Compact was signed on November 11, 1620, establishing the first equal rights contract under the division and power of the God of Christianity. This same contract was later incorporated into the U.S. Constitution.

The Puritans left their homeland in pursuit of freedom. Fleeing the persecution and oppression they had faced in England, they were determined to establish "holy commonwealths" in a new area, free from the tyrannical rule of James I and Charles I.[2] Most of the early settlers and English Puritans were devout Presbyterians who established church communities that reflected more individual authority instead of a hierarchal structure. In time, with the religious freedom and extension of several different communities influenced by the Plymouth Colony Separatists, many denominations thrived in the early part of America

(Anglicanism, Catholicism, and Puritanism).

From the Mayflower Compact to the Charter of Liberties strong religious convictions and personal striving for individual freedom characterized the colonists. This unwavering commitment to their Christian faith is what made America known for its rich Christian heritage.

The Great Awakening

As America continued to prosper, a mighty spiritual movement began to unfold. Strengthening the public and private life of Americans during the mid-seventeenth century, the Great Awakening began to shape American Protestantism and gave it new meaning in its role to the State. The many conversions that were authenticated during this religiously historic period changed the tone and nature of America altogether. Americans were not just theologically confirmed by an ecclesiastical body, but were now experiencing true Christianity lived out through the power of the gospel and work of the Holy Spirit. Jonathan Edwards (1703–1755) and George Whitefield (1714–1770) are widely acknowledged as the most influential figures in the Great Awakening. Their sermons covered the holiness of God, heaven and hell, and sin and salvation in startling ways unheard of by prior clergymen. Through their dynamic preaching, America experienced thousands of people receiving salvation for the very first time. This awakening brought forth new Protestant sects (Baptist and Methodist) and spread Christianity throughout the colonies in America.

American history transparently shows the course, establishment, and inoculation of Christianity in early colony life. Throughout the years, our Christian heritage has played a significant role in *who* we are and *what* we believe. That is, until now. In our present age, we have become unsure of our faith, muddled in our standards and unclear in what has truly defined American history. We have shifted away from our Christian heritage and gradually entered into a post-Christian era.

CHAPTER 2

Threat #1: Remove God

"Say to them, 'This is the nation whose people will not obey the LORD their God and who refuse to be taught. Truth has vanished from among them; it is no longer heard on their lips.'"[1] Jeremiah 7:28

R egrettably, the Christian heritage has been in decline in America for quite some time. Chuck Colson referred to this disengagement from God as a "post-Christian" culture that "no longer relies on Judeo-Christian truths as the basis of their public philosophy or their moral consensus. This is a significant cultural shift. At the birth of our nation, no one—not even deists and skeptics—doubted that basic biblical truths undergirded American institutions and defined the nation's values. Though the Founders drew heavily from Enlightenment philosophy as well as from Christian tradition, few at the time saw any contradiction between the two. And for most of our nation's history, these basic truths remained the foundation of the social consensus."[2]

Post-Christian Era

America is experiencing moral, political, and social bewilderment due to the attacks against God spread throughout the culture. God and prayer have been removed from schools, and the Pledge of Allegiance is under attack for being unconstitutional.[3] From inception, the pledge was solidified to be a patriotic oath as well as a public prayer. President Eisenhower signed the Pledge of Allegiance into law, stating, "In this way we are reaffirming the transcendence of religious faith in America's heritage and future; in this way we shall constantly strengthen those spiritual weapons which forever will be our country's most powerful resource, in peace or in war."[4]

This secularized takeover points to a growing hatred towards God in America as well as the determination to remove belief and dependence of God altogether. The attempt to remove God is the principal threat to our faith, families and country, and unfortunately, one that is gaining momentum. The stirring movement for a godless nation is getting worldwide exposure from several outspoken atheists.[5] These atheists are prolific authors and speakers who make it their highest aim to expose religion, particularly Christianity, as a sham. It is reasonable to assume that they not only reject Christian claims, they despise Christianity. A particularly successful method of doing this is to indoctrinate America in the worldview of Naturalism.

Naturalism explains the origin of life through a mechanism of evolutionary processes. It interprets life as nothing more than an accidental combustion of atomic and subatomic elements. In essence, according to naturalism, our way of life is determined by nothing more than meaningless and unintelligible matter, not by an intelligent designer (Creator) who created and sustains all things. In a naturalistic worldview, there is neither the necessity of life nor a supreme value on life. That is to say, everything came about simply by mindless accident.

As our children file into their classrooms each morning and our young adults take their seats in universities, naturalism is spoon fed straight into their minds and hearts. It is a deadly but powerful weapon meant to eradicate whatever truth has been previously planted. Once indoctrinated, the young minds of the next generation are more likely to reject the God of their forefathers and espouse a new belief that human beings determine their own meaning, purpose and destiny of life. If these naturalistic ideas triumph, they will affect the way we think about the world and become the ruling law that will shape our families, cities, and culture at large. Through the insidious influence of naturalism, our nation's moral fabric that was founded on Judeo-Christian ethics — is rapidly decaying.[6]

If we do not submit to God's authority then man is free to choose and act however he deems appropriate. One only has to take a closer look at Russia, China, and North Korea to learn a thing or two about how anti-God viewpoints have played an integral role in shaping communist countries. Even the staunch German atheist, Friedrich Nietzsche (1844–1900), conceded the point that without God, the fate of the human race is self-destruction.[7] If a sold-out atheist like Nietzsche can admit the moral dangers of removing God from society, why is America entertaining the idea?

Disconnected Home

The first fallen blockade in this anti-God attack is in our own homes. The only surefire method for retaliating against this false propaganda is truth. But sadly, our children are given a fragmented worldview at best; a piecing together of biblical truths passed down to them by parents who are unsure of truth themselves. Shaping children with a biblical worldview in the home has become ambiguous or non-existent. The reason so many parents are not training their children in the ways of God is because they are biblically illiterate. How can they train their children if they have never been trained with a proper biblical worldview themselves?

Christians have become "too busy" to actually study

the Bible. Upon cracking open its pages, many feel they are met with a befuddlement of words and phrases that are difficult to understand, much less apply to modern day life. Researchers George Gallup and Jim Castelli state: "Americans revere the Bible–but, by and large, they don't read it. And because they don't read it, they have become a nation of biblical illiterates."[8]

This has been the cause of so many problems on many different levels. Biblical illiteracy impacts roles in marriage; the way parents raise their children; and will shape a child's worldview in society. Fathers, in particular, have struggled in their development of a biblical worldview, and (in many regards) vacated their God-given role as spiritual leaders in the home. This disconnection in the home is all rooted in spiritual superficiality and has resulted in parents becoming inadequate in instructing their children in spiritual truths and matters (1 Thess. 2:11-12; Eph. 6:4).

Compromised Churches

The second fallen blockade has clearly been our churches. I have had the privilege of serving as a pastor for several years. In my tenure, I have witnessed the frightful disconnect that many churches have with their families, and the total disregard to equip them for the work of the ministry (Eph. 4:12; Heb. 10:24-25; Tit. 3:1). Going to church is rare in professing Christian homes today, let alone gathering as a unified family to enrich themselves through biblical devotions. Young people, who once labeled themselves as "church-goers," are now riddled with doubt because their parents failed to teach and model a life fueled by faith.

The local church is not accurately addressing the problems in the home or the mass exodus of young people from the faith. They lack a strategic plan of action to engage the minds of our youth and to equip parents to properly train up their children in the way they should go. Churches today are increasingly more concerned with entertaining students rather than training them in topics related to the Word of God (moral standards, convictions and values). One would think that churches would make it a top priority to shepherd and equip families on how to strengthen their faith in the onslaught of our current culture (Gal. 4:3; Eph. 4:14-16; 1 Jn. 2:15-17). Instead, it is more common to find ministers who place a high priority on performing "the next best thing" rather than informing their students of the latest dangers that can (and will) wreck their lives.

Troubled Generation

The final fallen blockade that has cleared the path for the rising anti-God movement is evident all around us. The pain and hurt represented among this growing population of young people is palpable. In my experience working with families, I have encountered many young people who struggle to relate and open up to their parents. Most young people will tell you that they are beyond frustrated with their parent's hypocrisy and argumentative approach to life. Rather than discussing relevant issues openly and constructively, they feel removed and distant from their parents, and all alone.[9]

The revolution to remove God from this troubled generation is a destructive force that aims to demolish the foundation of objective truth and replace it with artificial spirituality. The future fate of our children will amount to a morally lost generation if God is not their objective moral standard. *} Powerful statement*

In short, with the growing number of biblically illiterate parents unable to teach truth to their children, and the emergent church refusing to preach from the Bible, it's no wonder our children reject God, absolute truth, and the Bible. There are reasons as to why this is happening in our families, churches and society as a whole today, which we will explore further.

CHAPTER 3

Threat #2: Redefine Truth

"What is truth?"
John 18:38

T hroughout the ages, philosophers and academics alike have pondered the answer to one of life's greatest questions: *What is truth?* For centuries, truth was regarded in terms of being absolute, unchanging, and corresponding to reality.

However these concepts no longer apply in today's world. Truth, it would seem, is up for grabs. In a satirical jab at the rising debate over truth, political pundit Stephen Colbert mockingly coined a new word: *truthiness*. "Truthiness" included the notion that not only is everyone entitled to their own opinions, but their own facts. Facts matter not at all... perception is one's definitive truth.[1]

This definition reverberated across America as the media seized upon "truthiness" and rapidly became a key buzzword and hot topic. It was even chosen as the Word of the Year by the American Dialect Society in 2005 and Merriam-Webster Dictionary in 2006. What began as political satire was actually an accurate portrayal of what people really thought and believed about truth. It revealed the prevailing opinion that truth is nothing more than feeling or perception that can be defined and redefined at will by each individual. By accident or not, Colbert's "truthiness" pointed to an emerging battle for truth.

Cultural Relativism: The Changing Opinion of Truth

Digging its roots deep into contemporary American society is cultural relativism. A proponent of cultural relativism "maintains that there are no objective and universal moral norms and for that reason everyone ought to follow the moral norms of his or her own culture."[2] This may seem reasonable, but beneath it is a fatally flawed ideology that seeks to remove God from the heart of America and devolve truth to personal preference.[3] This means an individual is not governed by absolutes but by arbitrary taste or disposition of the moment. But when a society embraces the idea that there are no objective moral norms, people are left with no superior guidance and moral standards to live by, which can lead to anarchy and chaos.

This attitude that truth is nothing more than feeling is not only prevalent in our culture but also detrimental to society. Today's young people will become tomorrow's misguided leaders because they weren't taught to understand the fundamentals of absolute truth and have adopted the reigning cultural viewpoint. Whatever they feel or think is regarded as true simply because they feel or think it. Young people with little or no traditional religious background accept this by default.

Even American families of religious faith are experiencing a mass exodus of young people leaving the faith they grew up believing at home in exchange for the cultural view of religious pluralism (i.e., belief that all religious views are true).

If you follow current trends, it does not take long to see the tentacles of cultural relativism invading schools, politics and the media. The entertainment media scandalously promotes TV shows that celebrate immorality and indecent behavior, while networks seek to indulge students with the ideas of relativism and social tolerance. This is significant given the impact media has in the lives of young people. The entertainment industry acts as a guide that offers teenagers "maps of reality" that helps them formulate and interpret the meaning of life, values, attitudes, behavioral norms, and social and gender roles.[4] By the time young people enter college their whole childhood has been programmed to believe that truth is subjective, not objective. Unfortunately, these same young people have very little with which to defend their subjective view.

Now left to formulate their own opinions of truth and religion, less than one third of teens believe that *one* religion is true, and more than 60 percent are convinced that *many* religions are true.[5] The majority of American teenagers today hold to a form of religious relativism. Deciding not to "judge" or "choose" or "decide" but rather "tolerate" and embrace those around them. It's not cool or accepted to hold to one essential belief, but to accept that all beliefs are essentially true.

The Consequence of Ideas

Tragically, we live in a world that values the gratification of self above all else. A society that negates absolute truth results in the indulgence of all things narcissistic. Our culture is erroneously mistaken to believe that we (mere humans) can change truth to our liking. The attainment of individual autonomy where an individual does what is right in his or her own eyes has resulted in moral chaos and has led to higher divorce rates, children born out of wedlock, and an enormous rise of violence in the home. Self-gratification within our culture grows ever so deep with the exploitation of women and children. Pornography accounts for the highest revenue of entertainment today and is responsible for ruining marriages, families, pastors, and prominent politicians.[6] Shapiro charts this moral decline by asserting, "Society told the porn generation that final moral authority rests inside each of us—and in our vanity, we listened."[7] The more desensitized our society becomes; the greater chance our future generation will become spiritually dilapidated in the end. *Powerful Statement*

CHAPTER 4

Threat #3: Replace Christianity

"A society which is predominately Christian will propagate Christianity through its schools: one which is not, will not."[1] C.S. Lewis

Tolerance, which was once understood to mean "putting up with something you don't necessary like," has been replaced with a more diversified form that espouses that all *paradox* views are equally valid – and it is wrong to object otherwise. This redefined view has become a potent weapon wielded by cultural relativists to convince the American public that tolerance ought to be embraced as the highest value in our society. This intellectual devolution has brought considerable destruction to the traditional Christian morals and is reshaping the American life with moral passivity and indifference. Overall, our society is shifting towards a personalized truth and an unorthodox form of living.

Behind the mask of tolerance lies a destructive ideology that rejects all objective truth, morals and absolute standards. Tolerance of this brand is a byproduct of cultural relativism. This new ideology is steadily replacing absolute truth, moral values and duties. If America remains on this course, there will be no place for truth at all; no place for absolutes; no place for Christianity; and certainly no place for the ultimate truth of God's Word, the Bible.

In addition, tolerance advocates pluralism. Pluralism holds to a diversity of truth that believes all views are true

← Paradox

in a multicultural society (despite whether they agree or oppose each other). The assumption is that there is no ultimate purveyor of absolute truth. This is where tolerance gets its traction. People can believe whatever they want to as long as they're being tolerant. Thus, anyone who claims to possess the right viewpoint is intolerant.

This is precisely the claim against Christianity. Many religious pluralists would say that Christianity is intolerant and a divisive religion that makes radically biased statements. To think that Jesus is the "only way" is an absurd proposition of religious bigotry that only produces strife. Some non-Christians say that Christianity is an intolerant religion that espouses racism, sexism or imperialism.[2] Other non-Christians feel that Christianity is too restrictive and prevents people from naturally expressing their hedonistic desires and freedoms. Our current culture may bask in the freedom that includes the right to believe in religious pluralism, but it seemingly abhors commitment to one exclusive religion.

Though society appears to be tolerant of religion and its free exercise, in this post-Christian era of naturalism and cultural relativism, Judeo-Christian truths are rejected as an objective moral basis of public policy, legislation and viewpoints.[3] Religious expressions (particularly Christian) are heavily restricted and deemed unconstitutional. What once undergirded the formation of our nation and its values is no longer accepted in any public domain. This attempt to privatize faith and remove its influence in public life is succeeding in silencing and slowly replacing Christianity altogether.

Separation Doctrine: "America shalt not worship."

In 1830, upon arriving to North America from France, Alexis de Tocqueville wrote, "The religious aspect of the country was the first thing that struck my attention; and the longer I stayed there, the more I perceived the great political consequences resulting from this new state of things. In France I had almost always seen the spirit of religion and the spirit of freedom marching in opposite directions. But in America I found they were intimately united and that they reigned in common over the same country."[4] The Constitution of North Carolina (1776) proclaims that: "...all men have a natural and unalienable right to worship Almighty God according to the dictates of their own consciences."[5]

It is astonishing to think that despite all the evidence indicating our nation was founded on Judeo-Christian truths, America continues to reject the obvious. Many of the secular advancements to replace religious discussion from the public square come from employing "separation of church and state" and the First Amendment as legal principles penned by Jefferson. Secularists (non-religious) want us to believe that Jefferson allegedly supported the idea that there was no place for any religious reference among citizenry and that religious disturbance was not to be tolerated in the public affairs of life. They promote these false views and misrepresentation of the facts because they want us to buy into the lie that America has always been a secular nation. However, contrary to popular belief, what we actually find in history is quite a different story regarding Jefferson's viewpoints and the role Christianity played in shaping America. With historical objectivity as our guide, let us settle the truth about the "separation of church and state" once and for all.

Who Phrased the Infamous Phrase?

In reference to the phrase "a wall of separation between church and state," we can indeed attribute that to Thomas Jefferson. However, we must do so in the proper context. Jefferson was not the originator of this phrase, but it was actually used as a famous metaphor by ministers in England in the 1500s, and eventually in America in the 1600s. After periods of state control and corruption of religion, an early Methodist bishop by the name of Charles Galloway insisted that there ought not be any intrusion of governmental matters with ecclesiastical ones. Rev. Richard Hooker was actually the first to use the phrase, "separation of...Church and Commonwealth" under the reign of King Henry VIII of England. The phrase "separation of church and state" originated from the Pilgrims' religious flight from England under the ecclesiastical supremacy of Queen Elizabeth. The Pilgrims fled to Holland and eventually settled in America where they stressed that government had no right to "compel religion, to plant churches by power, and to force a submission to ecclesiastical government by laws and penalties."[6] Therefore, the purpose of separation was always to protect the church from interference by the government – not to protect the government from the church.

What Did Our Founders Believe?

The First Amendment is essentially divided up into two clauses. The first being the *Establishment Clause*: "Congress shall make no law respecting an establishment of religion;" and the second being the *Free Exercise Clause*: "or prohibiting the free exercise thereof; or abridging the freedom of speech, or of the press; or the right of the people peaceably to assemble, and to petition the Government for a redress of grievances." What exactly is the intended meaning of words like "establishment," "religion," "prohibit," and "free exercise?"

The Framers made it abundantly clear from the start that *Congress*, not individual states, is limited in its capacity to establish, exercise, and even disestablish a state-run religion. Additionally, the Establishment Clause is the one that prohibits Congress from having jurisdiction or enforcement over the religious freedoms expressed in public life, and, it is the Free Exercise Clause that allows the state (i.e., Congress) to protect these religious freedoms and expressions. Historically speaking, the view of that day was that the Church (religion) and State (government) were two separate spheres but with adjoined purposes. Government was to protect the civility *for* the people. Religion was to enhance the morality and vitality *of* the people.

On July 13, 1787, the Continental Congress enacted the Northwest Ordinance, and in it they prodigiously professed: "Religion, morality and knowledge, being necessary to good government and the happiness of mankind, schools and the means of education shall be forever encouraged."[7] Those in attendance included George Washington, James Madison, Alexander Hamilton, and Benjamin Franklin. These men are considered the most prominent figures in the development of the U. S. Constitution and the ratification of the Bill of Rights. George Washington was not only the President of the Convention which created the U.S. Constitution, but he was also the President of the United States who pushed for the creation of the Bill of Rights to enhance the principles and protections of the liberties expressed in the U.S. Constitution. We find no mentioning of a privatized faith of any sort in Washington's writings or addresses to the American people.

What Did Jefferson Believe?

It's important to point out that though Jefferson was the architect of the Declaration of Independence, he was not a framer of the U.S. Constitution.[8] Jefferson was in France (acting as Ambassador) at the time of the writing of the U.S. Constitution and the Bill of Rights. On June 19, 1802, Jefferson wrote a letter in response to an article he had received from Dr. Joseph Priestly who accredited the success of the U.S. Constitution to him. Jefferson wrote:

> One passage in the paper you enclosed me
> must be corrected. It is the following, 'And
> all say it was yourself more than any other
> individual, that planned and established it,'
> i. e., the Constitution. I was in Europe when
> the Constitution was planned, and never
> saw it till after it was established. [9]

Upon Jefferson becoming President in 1801, many Baptists were strong supporters of his Anti-Federalist positions and sought counsel from the President. They did so based upon the reading of the Kentucky Resolution of 1798 whereby Jefferson declared his beliefs of interpreting the U.S. Constitution:

> That it is true as a general principle, and is
> also expressly declared by one of the amend-
> ments to the Constitutions, that "the powers
> not delegated to the United States by the
> Constitution, our prohibited by it to the
> States, are reserved to the States respectively,
> or to the people"; and that no power over the
> freedom of religion, freedom of speech, or
> freedom of the press being delegated to the
> United States by the Constitution, nor pro-
> hibited by it to the States, all lawful powers
> respecting the same did of right remain, and
> were reserved to the States or the people:
> that thus was manifested their determination
> to retain to themselves the right of judging
> how far the licentiousness of speech and of
> the press may be abridged without lessening
> their useful freedom, and how far those

abuses which cannot be separated from their
use should be tolerated, rather than the use
be destroyed....[10]

According to this and other public remarks by Jefferson,
the Danbury Baptists knew the President opposed governmental control and interference in religious matters of the
church. In October 7, 1801, the Danbury Baptist Association
of Connecticut wrote to President Jefferson about their concern that religious liberty is a God-given right, not a privilege granted by the government. They realized that if the
government granted such religious freedoms to the people,
then that would mean that it could, at any given time,
remove them. In response to the Danbury Baptists, Jefferson
replied on January 1, 1802:

> Believing with you that religion is a matter
> which lies *solely* between man and his God,
> that he *owes account to none other for his faith
> or his worship*, that the legislative powers of
> government reach *actions only*, and *not opin-
> ions*, I contemplate with sovereign rever-
> ence that act of the whole American people
> which declared that their *legislature* would
> "make no law respecting an establishment
> of religion, or prohibiting the free exercise
> thereof," thus building a wall of separation
> between Church and State. Adhering to this
> expression of the *supreme will* of the nation
> in behalf of the *rights of conscience*, I shall
> see with sincere satisfaction the progress
> of those sentiments which tend to *restore* to
> man all his *natural rights*, convinced he has
> *no natural right in opposition to his social duties*
> [emphasis mine].[11]

On subsequent occasions, Jefferson articulated this same position to others as he did to the Danbury Baptists. Jefferson wrote, "I consider the government of the U.S. as interdicted by the constitution from intermeddling with religious institutions, their doctrines, discipline, or exercises. This results not only from the provision that no law shall be made respecting the establishment, or free exercise of religion, but from that also which reserves to the states the powers not delegated to the U.S."[12] John Adams agreed with Jefferson, stating, "We have no government armed with power capable of contending with human passions unbridled by morality and religion . . . Our Constitution was made only for a moral and religious people. It is wholly inadequate to the government of any other."[13] Jefferson and the Danbury Baptists were simply addressing the dangers of the government's marginalizing religious freedoms, not the other way around. Once again, it is perfectly clear that the separation doctrine was a campaign of the church to remove government oversight, not the government trying to remove the church from public life.

When Did It Become Misinterpreted?

In 1878 the U.S. Supreme Court used Jefferson's "separation" metaphor as part and parcel to the ruling that it is the government's duty to protect rather than limit the free exercise of religious preference. In fact, the Court took it a step further by invoking Jefferson's famous Virginia Act of Religious Freedom of 1786 in order to point out a few exceptions whereupon the government does have authority to intervene on religious matters. David Barton interprets the Court's ruling of Jefferson's statute as such:

> That Court (and others) then identified a handful of actions that, if perpetrated in the

name of religion, the government did have legitimate reason to limit, including bigamy, concubinage, incest, child sacrifice, infanticide, parricide, and other similar crimes. But the government was *not* to impede traditional religious expressions in public, such as public prayer, public display of religious symbols, public use of Scriptures, acknowledgement of God in public events, and so on. In short, the separation of Church and State existed not to remove or secularize the free exercise of religion but rather to preserve and protect it, regardless of whether it was exercised in private or public life.[14]

Thus, according to the Founders, religion played a virtuous role in shaping the values of a nation governed by the moral character *of* the people and *for* the people.

And yet in a landmark decision by the U.S. Supreme Court in 1947, the High Court declared that the Establishment Clause of the First Amendment not only applied to the imposed limitations of the federal government, but to States as well. Justice Black openly declared, "In the words of Jefferson, the clause against establishment of religion by law was intended to erect 'a wall of separation between Church and State.'" [15]

Over a century and a half later, the U.S. Supreme Court seized Jefferson's phrase "wall of separation" and applied an anti-religious interpretation to the First Amendment. It was no longer a safeguard from intrusion or obstruction on the part of Congress, but now a flipped version that merged the Establishment Clause of the First Amendment with the due process law of the Fourteenth Amendment that fundamentally changed the course of religion in public life. Since the pronouncement by the U.S. Supreme Court in 1947, almost every case addressing religious and public separation cite Jefferson as the architect of both the First Amendment and the law of "separation of church and state."

However, as already shown, this is not only a fabrication of American history, but it's also a poor rendering of the First Amendment. Spalding clarifies, "What this reconciliation of religion and politics did not mean is equally important, and crucial to understanding the meaning and significance of religious liberty: This official separation of church doctrine and the new federal government never meant—was never intended to imply—the separation of religion and politics, or the expunging of religion from public life."[16] That's precisely why former Chief Justice, William Rehnquist (served 1986-2005), admittedly observed, "The metaphor of a wall of separation is bad history and worse law. It has made a positive chaos out of court rulings. It should be explicitly abandoned."[17]

Based on the examination of the origin and historical meaning of the separation doctrine, it's obvious that it has always been the government who has jumped the "wall of separation" and not the Church. But because of the mishandling of our Founders' religious (mainly Christian) viewpoints, particularly those of Jefferson, and robbing government of its proper role to protect religion in public life, secularism has altered the course of American history. As a result, secularism has been widely successful in removing God, redefining truth, and is well on its way to replacing Christianity.

CHAPTER 5

Taking Back Our Faith

"Contend for the faith that was once for all entrusted to the saints." Jude 3

Let me be clear, the longer Christians stay divided on issues and remain stagnant on solutions, the sooner Christianity will become obsolete in America. There can be no more complacency, passivity, and apathy. It is going to take more than a few pundits arguing their side and trying to sell their views on the news. If we are going to take back our faith from secularism, we must rise up together in action.

Seek God

In order to preserve and expand Christianity in our country once again, we must do what our Founders did when they knelt together in prayer at the Constitutional Convention in Philadelphia (1787) and sought God for wisdom, guidance and fortitude. Thereafter was drafted the seventeen page document known today as the Constitution of the United States of America.

These brave Founders were brilliant idealists fueled with a passionate dream to see common men liberated from tyranny and placed on the path of divine freedom ordained by God. Despite their various theological and denominational disagreements, the Founders exercised great strength and determination to set aside their differences and agree on the fundamental belief that God was the origin of their existence and Jesus Christ was the Savior of the world. This characterized our Founders and united a resilient desire to build a nation on the God-given liberties that sparked a revival among Christians and spread the gospel throughout American history.

That same pursuit of God that our Founders had must be reignited in us. We must seek God and be willing to meet the needs of others above our own. This takes a humble heart before God and true repentance of our sins. Remember these words spoken by God to Solomon, "If my people, who are called by my name, will humble themselves and pray and seek my face and turn from their wicked ways, then will I hear from heaven and will forgive their sin and will heal their land (2 Chr. 7:14)."

As Christians pray, they need to become better acquainted with the nature and attributes of God. There are many Christians who believe Jesus is God and Savior, but are lacking in their view of who God really is. One's view of God is a central element. If anyone is to grow spiritually their concept of God must align with the Bible and recognize that He is the Ultimate Standard of truth and meaning of life (Rev. 1:8).

So who is God? God is the Most High who has sovereign control and supreme power over heaven and the inhabitants on earth (Ps. 22:28; 103:19; 135:5-6). He alone is the Creator and Sustainer over everything that has its existence according to His complete purpose and will (Isa. 40:28; Eph. 1:11). In essence, God (who is absolutely free) has the absolute right to execute His universal authority over His creation and not a single thing in His creation can impede His purposes (Ps. 115:3).

The Bible teaches that God is Self-Existent (Ex. 3:14; Deut. 6:4). He is eternal and immutable; there is no beginning or end to Him and He cannot change within His perfect and complete existence (Deut. 33:27; Heb. 6:17-18). Though God's creation is in constant flux, He is eternally perfect with no potency to change. God is also an Infinite Being (Ps. 147:5; Isa. 66:1) who is limitless and boundless and everything that exists proceeds from Him. A. W. Tozer stated it this way, "There is nothing boundless but God and nothing infinite but God. God is self-existent and absolute; everything else is contingent and relative. There is nothing very big and nothing very wise and nothing very wonderful. It's all relatively so. It is only God who knows no degrees."[1] Thus, God experiences no growth or improvement from His perfectly infinite nature. He is fully capable of holding and sustaining everything together by His infinite power (Ex. 6:3). Therefore, everything outside of God is dependent on Him for existence because He has existed for all eternity.

This is the great God that we seek and serve. He is the Holy One who has given us our most precious faith and will preserve it until He returns (1 Pet. 1:4-5). J.I. Packer writes, "God is a tripersonal Being who so loves ungodly humans that the Father has given the Son, the Son has given his life, and Father and Son together now give the Spirit to save sinners from unimaginable misery and lead them into unimaginable glory. Believing in and being overwhelmed by this amazing reality of divine love generates and sustains the love to God and neighbor that Christ's two great commandments require (Matt. 22:35-40). Our love is to express our gratitude for God's gracious love to us, and model it in return (Eph. 4:32–5:2; 1 John 3:16)."[2]

As the body of Christ, we are called to unite together in the Spirit and unity of peace with the common goal to save our communities with the love and power of the gospel (Phil. 1:12-18). Imagine what would happen if Christians all across this great land returned to a right view of God and began to repent of their sins, restore the division in their churches, pray for the protection of their families, and heal the brokenness in their cities. This may be hard to visualize, but that's what is required to take back our faith!

Pursue Truth

As a Christian, knowing who God is enables you to know truth as well (Ps. 119:160). Truth cannot be redefined but is defined and established by God as a universal standard for all to obey and follow. However, this is not a view held by most Americans. If Christians want to stop the moral decline in their nation, they need to wake up to the reality that the next generation has adopted opinions that are drastically contrary to Christianity. That's why Christians need to be engaged in the battle and voice their concerns and take part in strengthening and preserving the truth given by God.

First, you must *think* before you *believe*. Generally speaking, most Christians do not give much thought to what they believe. This is of great importance because the Proverb teaches, "as a man thinks in his heart so he is." Consequently, a person's beliefs or worldview—how one makes sense of God and life—will either be comprised of arbitrary opinions (that hold no real significance) or of absolute standards from the Word of God (that contain real substance and meaning).

Here is a simple acrostic that will help you remember what is T.R.U.E. about truth (Ps. 19:1-3; Rom. 1:18-20):

> **Transcendent** – God is truth and has revealed His truth to mankind. Truth existed prior to anyone's knowledge of it. Take gravity for example. Gravity existed prior to the discovery of Newton. Likewise, humans did not determine the nature of truth; they

simply discovered the meaning of it by God.
Real – Truth corresponds to reality (thought, belief, statement). Simply put, truth is telling it like it is. For example, either I'm married or a bachelor. I can't be both at the same time and in the same sense. Otherwise, it would be a contradiction because the facts don't match up to the real world (truth).

Universal – Truth is for all people, at all times and in all locations. For example, 2+2=4 is universally true and applied by everyone, everywhere and at all times.

Exclusive – Truth is absolute and exclusive. That is to say, truth never changes even though our beliefs about truth change. It was always true that the earth was round even though people believed it to be flat. The truth *is*; what people think is true does not change what is absolutely true.

With a proper understanding of truth, you will be able to think critically and therefore dismantle the dangerous philosophy of relativism. For example, if someone believes that truth is relative, you ask, "Is that absolutely true?" If they say "no" (deny), then they are admitting that their statement is not true (i.e., it's false). If they say "yes" (affirm), then they are agreeing against their own statement (i.e., contradiction). Either way, it exposes relativism as self-defeating because one must hold to an absolute truth in order to assert it as true in the first place — which is nonsensical.

Second, do not underestimate or undervalue the convictions of your faith. God has given every person a set of convictions about certain values about the reality and purpose of life (Rom. 2:14-15). Many well-meaning Christian families gradually slip into complacency when it comes to living out their faith and moral values. Left unchecked, complacency eventually begins to erode the foundation and opens the door to ignorance, which (in the end) will destroy your faith.

Third, spend more time growing in the truth of God's word as a family. The apostle Peter wrote, "Like newborn infants, long for the pure spiritual milk, that by it you may grow up into salvation (1 Pet. 2:2)." With the increasing tendency of young people defining and fashioning their own personal truth and belief system, parents must be trained and equipped to teach their families the truths of God and equip them to do the same.

Fourth, learn how to effectively spread God's truth using all forms of communication. You can't allow the cultural media to drown out your Christian voice. Be diligent to pursue the knowledge of God and share these truths through various channels in social networking, blogs, books, websites, and purpose driven seminars. America needs more Christians who are willing to learn and help others learn as well.

Defend the Faith

The command to defend the faith is one that is prominently displayed in the Bible (Acts 22:1; 25:8; 1 Cor. 9:3; 2 Cor. 7:11; Phil. 1:7; 2 Tim. 4:16). The most quoted verse on the defense of the faith is found in 1 Peter 3:15, "But in your hearts set apart Christ as Lord. Always be prepared to give an answer [*defense*] to everyone who asks you to give the reason for the hope that you have. But do this with gentleness and respect." The word "defense" is the Greek word *apologia*, which literally means, "to speak away." Thus, the study of apologetics teaches Christians how to defend against false views while preserving the credibility and objective truth of the Christian faith.

This is extremely important considering how many Christians are biblically illiterate and inactive in sharing their faith with others. As a Christian, you are called to defend the faith and engage the culture for Christ (Eph. 6:19, 20). As you learned the truth behind the separation doctrine, you cannot allow the lies perpetuated by the secular world to deter you from publically and unashamedly sharing your faith (Rom. 1:16).

Today's generation doesn't know any better. The extent of their teaching is that it's unconstitutional and inappropriate to openly display their faith in public. But as mentioned previously, our Founders endorsed and pursued this nation to be a religious one whereby all Americans can live a free and moral life. They made a clear distinction in the U.S Constitution of what religious freedom *is* and *ought not* to be. They underscored that there be no place for a dominant government or sectarian religion with overriding power to legislate law according to its own secular or religious edicts.[3] Church and State were both meant to coexist in an adjoining fashion to bring out the moral best in private, as well as in public life. For example, Washington not only displayed how his faith impacted his public life, but he emphasized how important religious principles are in guiding our private lives as well.[4]

It is out of the expressed tenets of the U.S. Constitution that the Founders agreed on these most fundamental principles:

1. The Church is a proper authority that the state must respect.
2. The federal government should neither prohibit the free exercise of religion nor establish an official religion of the State.
3. Every person should enjoy religious liberty.
4. Religion is vital to the survival and prosperity of the

American Experiment.
5. We know by reason that God and natural law exist.
6. Public displays of respect for God are right and good, and don't constitute an establishment of religion.[5]

Therefore, the public and free exercise of religion is legal and is supported by the U.S. Constitution. If America plans to return to its historical roots of liberty and morality then faith (religion) and reason (experience) must be intrinsically woven into the fabric of our society both privately and publically. I encourage you to dig deeper into Christianity and take some courses in theology, evangelism and apologetics. There are amazing resources out there that can help build confidence in evangelizing the gospel and preparing you with a holistic worldview.[6]

It is up to you to teach the next generation to seek God, pursue truth and defend the faith. Take a moment and reflect on how you believe your Christian faith has shaped the next generation in America.

PART TWO

The War To Destroy
Our Family

CHAPTER 6

Family: The Heart of America!

*"This is all the inheritance I can give my dear family.
The religion of Christ can give them one which will
make them rich indeed."[1]* Patrick Henry

The English Puritan clergyman Thomas Manton (1620-1677) wrote, "A family is the seminary of the church and state and if children be not well principled (taught) there, everything will go wrong."[2] The Puritans who came to America strongly believed that the home was the primary place to educate and disciple their children according to the teachings of the Bible. The great American theologian, Jonathan Edwards (1703-1758) said, "Every Christian family ought to be as it were a little church, consecrated to Christ, and wholly influenced and governed by his rules. And family education and order are some of the chief means of grace."[3]

Family Life

The early colonists sought to raise a family that exemplified biblical faith and values, which would be multiplied throughout future generations. These guidelines were taken directly from the passage of Deuteronomy 6:6, 7: "These commandments that I give you today are to be upon your hearts. Impress them on your children. Talk about them when you sit at home and when you walk along the road, when you lie down and when you get up." This wasn't simply a duty, but a God-ordained command.

Moreover, the Puritans (English Protestants) saw the family as the highest social institution given by God, and to be the primary function to build the church and government. The Puritan pastor and theologian Richard Baxter wrote:

> We must have a special eye upon families, to see that they are well ordered, and the duties of each relation performed. The life of religion, and the welfare and glory of both the Church and the State, depend much on family government and duty. If we suffer the neglect of this, we shall undo all.... I beseech you, therefore, if you desire the reformation and welfare of your people, do all you can to promote family religion.[4]

The Puritans were passionate believers in establishing a "visible" Kingdom of God, a society that exemplified an honest, civil and faith-based life in the family, church and state.[5] By the 1700s, small communities were established, and many Puritan and Quaker (Religious Society of Friends) homes adopted particular customs and lifestyles reflected from the Bible. They strongly believed marriage to be a fundamental social institution established by God to build healthy and prosperous families through the physical and spiritual relationship between a husband and wife.

There was a specific structure modeled in these homes. The father represented the head of the home and worked hard on the farm or exercised a particular craft or trade to provide financial income for the family. It is said of women in the colonial period that they exercised no power. That applied to ownership of land (when married) and legal action, but certainly not when it came to the domestic affairs of her household.[6] The mother worked tirelessly as she reared the children, cooked the meals, sewed and cleaned the clothes, educated the children, and aided her husband on various duties related to his work.

The children played an intricate role as well. Depending on the land settled upon, the family required every member from the age of three and onward to play a meaningful role. The children conducted much of the hard work cultivating, planting and harvesting the crops and feeding the animals.[7] The contributions from the family unit ensured the family's welfare and provided additional resources for the family. Life in the early colonies brought a strong sense of hard work, community and dependence upon one another.

In an age that experienced a high mortality rate among parents and children, it was essential that parents worked to fulfill their distinctive roles and bring about the most stability and security for their family. It was customary for extended relatives to take in and rear and educate children who lost their parents. This speaks of the strong value the family played in building and strengthening, not only the person, but the community at large.

The early settlers were not focused on individual gain, but were determined to give their children a better and brighter future than they could have ever achieved. Through an orderly process of education, hard work and spiritual preparation in the home, a strong foundation was being laid. This strong foundation afforded the future generations the opportunity to pursue and fulfill their dreams.

CHAPTER 7

Threat #1: Remove Family Structure

"The Spirit clearly says that in later times some will abandon the faith and follow deceiving spirits and things taught by demons." 1 Timothy 4:1

Once a strong beacon of hope in early America, the family model has now become fragmented and lacking in moral fortitude. Unfortunately, the present model holds only bits and pieces of what God designed and purposed it to be. This is what happens when rebellious people turn from God and want to live according to their own standards. This is what happens when sinful men mistakenly believe their ways are better than those of a perfect God.

Family Destruction

What are the ramifications of this philosophy? Who is affected by this dysfunction? Over 60 percent of Americans do not mind the new trends affecting the family structure. They may not approve of everything that goes on with homosexual couples, single moms/dads, and cohabitating couples raising a family, but overall they do not seem to be too concerned. With this commonplace apathy, our traditional family unit is increasingly sinking into oblivion.

Cultural relativism has been the deadly culprit, successfully erasing the lines of traditional marriage and effectively impacting the next generation. Relationships are approached with a noncommittal attitude rather than a marriage covenant. Add to that the growing number of people who view "cohabitating" together as an alternative to marriage; a "friends with benefits" relationship where couples live together, have sex, and do all the other things married couples do with no strings attached. Many Americans choose this form of living because it comes with very little commitment and they can opt out at any time. And why commit or get married when the divorce rate in America is staggering? It is estimated between 40 to 50 percent of marriages will end in divorce.[1] Simple change of preference or regret allows for these divorces. What once was unacceptable or disdained has become the norm.

These major drifts from traditionalism to a more "modernized" structure are forming a new level of dysfunctionalism in the family. John MacArthur lists a series of increased dysfunction due to the abandonment of Christ in the home:

> Over the past few generations, we have seen that destructive process taking place before our eyes. It seems contemporary secular society has declared war on the family. Casual sex is expected. Divorce is epidemic. Marriage itself is in decline, as multitudes of men and women have decided it's preferable to live together without making a covenant or formally constituting a family. Abortion is a worldwide plague. Juvenile delinquency is rampant, and many parents have deliberately abandoned their roles of authority in the family. On the other hand, child abuse in many forms is escalating. Modern and postmodern philosophies have attacked the traditional roles of men and women within the family.

Special interest groups and even government agencies seem bent on the dissolution of the traditional family, advocating the normalization of homosexuality, same-sex "marriage," and (in some cultures nowadays) sterilization programs. Divorce has been made easy, tax laws penalize marriage, and government welfare rewards childbirth outside of wedlock. All those trends (and many more like them) are direct attacks on the sanctity of the family.[2]

This break of the family structure has had devastating effects on families, the economy, criminal behavior, and education. According to the U.S. Census Bureau, one out of every three children lives in a home without a father. This is unsettling because standardized reports show that children who grow up without a father in the home are five times more likely to live in poverty.[3] How does the government intend to fix these issues? The National Fatherhood Initiative reports that the federal government spends a whopping 100 billion dollars every year on programs to help support children with absentee fathers.[4]

Though it may seem that spending large sums of taxpayer money helps, it only succeeds in making matters worse. The government has mistakenly shifted its attention from the backbone of our country, and has instead rewarded broken homes with welfare programs to aid their unending dysfunction. The truth is welfare programs do not address the root issues that bring families to their point of need in the first place.

Self-Individualism

Broken families stem from broken people. Unfortunately, the American philosophy today revolves around the individual rather than the family. What used to be a central focus and intent has now become secondary. Greed and the promotion of self are the motivators behind decisions. Americans want more money. Americans want fewer hassles. Americans want more time. Americans want more choices. Americans do not want any worries.[5] While the primary focus is on *self*, the effects are widespread. Rationalizing this mentality within the needs of the family only increases the pressure and focus on self. The inability to achieve success leads to worry and ultimately a sense of failure. The majority of Americans today are overly stressed and worried about their jobs, raising their families, the safety of their children, and paying down debt while planning for retirement so they can enjoy life before they die. The load of these concerns weighs down most Americans and if left untreated, can cause severe health risks such as heart disease, depression, high blood pressure, and sleep disorders--not to mention the emotional strain on the family.

As a pastor, I have seen first hand what self-individualism can do to the average family. It is sad to say, but many Christians living in America have gotten so wrapped up in what they want that they have neglected the responsibility to build up their family according to the teachings of the Word of God. Sports, activities, and social functions take precedence above all else. Married couples are too busy to spend time with each other, which leads to more frustration and arguments in the marriage. This leaves little time or inclination to read the Bible, disciple children, and serve in the church.

As precious as time is, many Christian families have allowed time to control their lives rather than using it to bring out the best in their families. Sadly, having a godly family based on biblical principles is not the priority. If this is true among Christian families, how much more so will it be true among society as a whole? The more dysfunctional and out of place the family structure becomes, the easier it is to remove altogether.

The Biblical Standard

One of the great failures in Christian homes today is the lack of spiritual investment parents have deposited into their children. Parents have succumbed to parenting on worldly standards rather than on biblical standards. They are so attentive to the success in grades, achievements in sports, and various accolades that they have forgotten that their primary goal is to "train up" their children in the ways of the Lord (Pro. 22:6). They have become so focused on *what* they want their children to become, that they have lost sight of *who* they will be in the future.

The Bible refers to three divinely organized institutions: (1) **family** (Gen. 2:18-24; Deut. 6:6-7; Ps. 127:3-5; Eph. 5:22-33); (2) **government** (Rom. 13; Tit. 3:1; 1 Pet. 2:13-14); and (3) the **church** (Matt. 16:18-19; Ac. 20:28; Col. 1:18). According to the Bible, the only institution (out of the three) given by God to train children is the home. The home is to be a safe environment that fosters learning and discipleship. It is to be the central stabilizing force to help children learn and grow through all the various issues of life. Several key biblical passages allude to this: "I have chosen Abraham so that he will direct his children and his household to keep the way of the Lord (Gen. 18:19);" "how from infancy you [Timothy] have learned the Scriptures (2 Tim. 3:15);" "Fathers...bring your children up in the training and instruction of the Lord (Eph. 6:4)." And, of course, Deuteronomy 6:7, "Impress them [God's laws] on your children. Talk about them when you sit at home and when you walk along the road, when you lie down and when you get up."

Accordingly, God gives parents the primary position to train their children up in the spiritual, moral and natural development. This is not to mean that parents are the only teachers, but that they are to be the primary teacher in establishing a biblical worldview in their child's life. Christians are not to solely rely on the church to disciple their children. Even more so, parents should not be allowing the government to serve as the primary influencers in the education, future career choices, and worldview development of their children. That is not their role; that is the role of parents. Therefore, based on the biblical mandate for a child's development, the social policies instituted by the federal government are an unnatural interference in this natural process within the family.

The Department of Education: "We own your kids."

Before proceeding, I want to make it clear that I am not taking issue with individual public school teachers. Many of my personal friends are public teachers who love their students and work extremely hard at educating and shaping young lives. I know many teachers who love what they do despite the lack of compensation and the very long hours. I admire them for their selfless devotion to their students, and I highly commend them!

With that in mind, I would like to address the overarching philosophy of the *system* of education, not necessarily the performance of educators (though that is partly the problem). I recognize this may cause several readers to feel uncomfortable or disagree. Nonetheless, I believe the direction our country has taken to educate our children has actually created more problems in the home and in the lives of our children. Therefore, I ask that Christians examine my arguments against the federal education system and make sure their families are not becoming part of the naturalistic system that seeks to indoctrinate their children.

The Education of Indoctrination

Why take issue with education? Why not another government system or department? The answer is this: whoever influences the education of our children controls the future of our nation. Abraham Lincoln said, "The philosophy in the schoolroom in one generation will be the philosophy of the government in the next."[6]

Consider the weight of this question: What power do you have over what your child learns in school? The answer is very little, if any at all. If parents were able to view the lesson plan from their child's teacher, they may not disapprove of most of the content. However, hidden in the subject matter is a methodology to secularize the hearts and minds of each student; a strategy to deconstruct whatever traditional, biblical teaching the child receives at home and replace it with naturalistic philosophy. It may sound dramatic but consider the history and progression of public education; where it started and where it is today.

For many centuries in Western civilizations, the belief in an omnipotent and omniscient Creator who created and sustains the universe was by far the accepted view scientifically, religiously and socially. Likewise, the foundation of the educational system in America was built around belief in a Creator God and the morals and values that came directly from the Bible. The critical role religion played in forming our educational system must not be de-emphasized.

In fact, the first schools in Massachusetts developed a booklet, *The New-England Primer,* which taught children the alphabet using Bible phrases and memorization of Scripture.[7] The first public school law ever passed in America was, "Old Deluder Satan Act" of 1646. This required all towns of 50 or more families to provide an elementary school, where teachers were required to teach, not only reading and writing, but the Bible as well. The Act declared, "It being one chief project of the old deluder, Satan, to keep men from the knowledge of the Scriptures . . . it is therefore ordered . . . [to] appoint one within their town to teach all such children as shall resort to him to write and read..."[8]

Well into the seventeenth century, the majority of our Founders championed the school to be a place to provide students the pleasure and opportunity to learn the Bible and Christianity. In 1749, Benjamin Franklin published a booklet on education. He emphasized the purpose of education to, "afford frequent opportunities of showing the necessity of a public religion . . . and the excellency of the Christian religion above all others."[9] James Monroe expressed, "An institution which endeavors to rear American youth in pure love of truth and duty, and while it enlightens their minds by ingenious and liberal studies, endeavors to awaken a love of country, to soften local prejudices, and *to inoculate Christian faith* and charity, cannot but acquire, as it deserves, the confidence of the wise and good [emphasis in original]."[10] It was Daniel Webster (famous statesman and lawyer) who appeared before the Supreme Court and argued, "The purest principles of morality are to be taught. Where are they found? Whoever searches for them must go to the source from which a Christian man derives his faith – the Bible."[11]

Over time, however, the educational system once grounded in teaching sound principles and biblical truths began to erode, and was gradually forged into a substantial platform for naturalistic philosophy. Today's educational system bears almost no resemblance to its former state and poses an enormous threat to the traditional family structure.

One wonders how education in our country could have shifted so radically from its inception. There were many prominent figures whose ideas strongly influenced this cultural shift. Listed below is a series of significant events that reshaped the form and purpose of American education.

- John Locke's (1632-1704), *An Essay Concerning Human Understanding* (1689) and *Some Thoughts Concerning Education* (1693) are main theses of empiricism (experience is the source of all knowledge) that taught against original sin and the need to educate children from a clean slate at birth.
- Jean Jacques Rousseau's (1712-1778) writing of *Émile* ("On Education," 1755) in France disseminated an educational system controlled by the government, not family. His later work *The Social Contract* (1762) argued that government has nothing to do with the will of God.
- By 1805 the Unitarians (religious liberalism) took over Harvard University (founded by Calvinists in 1636).
- G. W. F. Hegel (1770-1831) argued for a synthetic and ethical approach to education. In his book *Philosophy of Right* (1820-1821), Hegel argued for a totalitarian state to control people in a way that would enhance their quality and ethical life, and that parents should be forced to send their children to public education and have them 'vaccinated.' It is within the rights and duty of this controlled society to 'superintend' and 'influence' the shaping of the soul through education; which is paramount to a parent's influence over their children.
- Robert Owen (1771-1858) published *A New View of Society* (1816) that synthesized the Age of Enlightenment with the social change to bring about a "New World Order" or "New Institution" through the advancements of community schooling. Owen opened the New Institute for the Formation of Character; a revolutionary venture at New Lanark to

educate children within a controlled system.

- Robert Dale Owen (1801-1877), son of Robert Owen, published *Outline of the System of Education and New Lanark* (1824), which built on his father's legacy of reforming education by detailing a curriculum that brought forth the structure and layout of classrooms.

- Horace Mann (1796-1859) became the head of the newly formed Massachusetts State Board of Education (1837) and convinced the Whig Party (opposed Democrats) to legislate tax-supported elementary school education. He later adopted a Prussian model (state-controlled) of education in Germany that instituted compulsory attendance, national curriculum and testing. The plan was for the centralized government to shape the character of Americans.

- Charles Darwin (1809-1882) published *Origin of Species* (1859); his plausible theory of evolution relegated the supernatural (i.e., God) for naturalistic mechanisms of natural selection. It was not long afterward that the modernist culture began to accept the biological evolutionary framework in exchange for creation.

- Thomas Huxley (1825-1895; nicknamed "Darwin's Bulldog") advanced the theory of naturalism and became a great advocate and defender of Darwin's theory of natural selection. Huxley would later write *Evidence on Man's Place in Earth* (1863), which synthesized Darwin's work and made new extrapolations in the fields of paleontology, anthropology, embryology and literature. His extensive scientific output on evolution has had significant influence on subsequent education.[12]

- Karl Marx (1818-1883) co-authored *The Communist Manifesto* (1848) with Friedrich Engels (1820-1895) and went on to publish his first volume of *Das Kapital* (1867). Marxism began to replace more home education with a social education that centered on the philosophy of atheism, relativism and communism.

- In the decades preceding the Civil War, government became more centralized in education, and religion less prominent. By the 1870s, the Unitarians' adoption of the Prussian model and monopoly of education forced many private (Christian) schools to close down.
- William T. Harris (1835-1909) implemented progressive change to American education as the United States Commissioner of Education (1889-1906). He advocated more separation of church and state, and revolutionized high school education and school educators across America with relativism and humanism in his published work *The Philosophy of Education* (1906).
- Herbert Spencer's (1820-1903) work *Synthetic Philosophy* would be the first to take the construction of the evolutionary process and apply it to all branches of knowledge, such as: ethics, politics, law, psychology, biology, and sociology.[13]
- Stanley Hall (1844-1924) applied the theory of evolution to adolescent behavior and development, and published *Adolescence* (1904) and *Educational Problems* (1911).
- John Dewey (1859-1952) and his secular counterparts managed to become the major proponents of public education in America in the twentieth century. He campaigned for an education system centered on the belief that humans are nothing more than randomly assembled matter produced by unintelligible chance. This underlying denial of God gave teachers the authority to facilitate students in formulating their own set of moral and social constructs.

Over the last three centuries, the advancement of naturalism in academics has had enormous impact and has become a formidable opponent to biblical education throughout the schools and courtrooms in America. Since the Scopes Trial (1925), when the Butler Act forbade the teaching of the theory of evolution in schools, the federal courts have since rejected the idea of creationism being taught as an alternative to evolutionary education in public schools. Much of the success rests in the legal actions of the ACLU (American Civil Liberties Union) along with the help of the National Center for Science Education. They have been very successful in their cases before the U.S. Supreme Court, arguing that the biblical teaching of creationism is a "religious belief," not science, and prevented students from learning the scientific validity of evolution. Since religion is a matter of "separation of church and state," it is unconstitutional to teach creationism, and therefore, should have no place in the schools.[14]

This one-sided educational regime has made major headway in our educational system. It effectively indoctrinates our students with Darwinian evolution as "fact" and aims to provide them with the "correct" view of education, values and morality. The more our children are taught under the tutelage of the federal educational system and its underpinnings of naturalism, the more likely they will blindly accept and follow this philosophy in all areas of their lives. As Julian Huxley (1887-1975), a leading evolutionary biologist in his day, professed, "It is essential for evolution to become the central core of any educational system, because it is evolution, in the broad sense, that links inorganic nature with life, and the stars with earth, and matter with mind, and animals with man."[15] That was the goal of naturalists then and still today. Only today, that goal is nearly realized.

An Unconstitutional Education

The Department of Education undermines the Tenth Amendment, which states, "The powers not delegated to the United States by the Constitution, nor prohibited by it to the States, are reserved to the States respectively, or to the people." It is quite clear that the Tenth Amendment precludes the federal government from operating schools within sovereign states. The Framers were strong proponents of keeping education close to home, not manipulated and controlled by the federal government.

The truth is there are a total of thirty to thirty-five (depending how they are divided up) enumerated powers authorized to the federal government in the U.S. Constitution.[16] Education is not one of them. In actuality, there is absolutely no mention of the word "education" in the U.S. Constitution. As mentioned earlier, the Framers recognized the importance of education for children within their own community and therefore, did not include it on the federal level. This traditional philosophy was made clear in the early Northwest Ordinance of 1787 and 1789, which declared, "Religion, morality, and knowledge being necessary for good government and the happiness of mankind, schools and the means of learning shall forever be encouraged." This is historically significant, for under this ordinance, it was Congress's plan to distribute and allocate certain townships in states that had a parcel of land dedicated to public education.[17] This advocacy for moral and intellectual education for children was not based around the federal government, but centered on the family and community.

Eventually education became a presidential power play. However, the U.S. Constitution does not permit the President or Congress the authority to regulate education above state sovereignty.[18] Yet in 1980, President Jimmy Carter and Congress established the Department of Education as a Cabinet level agency, endorsed and backed by the two largest bureaucratic teacher unions: National Education Association (NEA) and the American Federation of Teachers (AFA) — effectively taking the power from individual states and parents![19] The late Albert Shanker (long time president of AFA) arrogantly conceded that the public education system operates as a "planned economy," and is "a bureaucratic system in which everybody's role is spelled out in advance and there are very few incentives for innovation and productivity."[20] Gregory Moo further points out in his book, *Power Grab*, how government monopoly puts its own interest first. He writes, "Monopolies that exist under law and receive funding through the taxing authority of governments — without regard to productivity — are breeding grounds for sprawling bureaucracies."[21]

This was not a campaign to *improve* the education of children as much as it was a *monopoly* on the education system. By placing education under one department, the President handed over an enormous amount of power to the teachers unions. Speaking at the 2009 NEA convention, former General Counsel Bob Chanin gave his farewell address. In his speech he proclaimed: "It is not because we care about children; and it is not because we have a vision of a great public school for every child. The NEA and its affiliates are effective advocates because we have power."[22] The enormous responsibility of shaping our young leaders is in the hands of skilled and boastful bureaucrats whose real achievement is to gain more power, not to love and educate children.

As a result, the public education structure has turned into a deliberate system that undermines parental rights and makes them subordinate to government controlled public schools. Much of the state and federal legislation blatantly undercuts parents' authority to decide what their children are exposed to once they enter the classroom. According to The Ninth Circuit of Appeals, "Although the parents are legitimately concerned with the subject of sexuality, there is no constitutional reason to distinguish that concern from any of the countless moral, religious, or philosophical objections that parents might have to other decisions of the School District."[23] A particular U.N. legislation ("The United Nations Convention For The Rights Of The Children") is attempting to shift parental responsibility into the control of the State. In article three of the U.N. Convention, it reads, "In all actions concerning children, whether undertaken by public or private social welfare institutions, courts of law, administrative authorities or legislative bodies, the best interests of the child shall be a primary consideration."[24] That is to mean, parents have no rights or power over the fundamental rights of their child or institutions that secure such rights. Most parents are unaware of these laws because the government wants parents to think their natural rights of custody and control are intact, when in fact, the government is the one with the actual power.

As parents continue to hand over the minds of their children to the public schools, many teachers look to inculcate these students in naturalism. The great American Presbyterian leader, A.A. Hodge (1823-1886) preached against the centralized educational system as a destructive mechanism conducted by an atheistic agenda:

> I am as sure as I am of the fact of Christ's reign that a comprehensive and centralized system of national education, separated from religion, as is now commonly proposed, will prove the most appalling enginery for the propagation of anti-Christian and atheistic unbelief, which this sin-rent world has ever seen... It is capable of exact demonstration that if every party in the State has the right of excluding from the public schools whatever he does not believe to be true, then he that believes the least must give way to him that believes absolutely

nothing, no matter how small a minority the atheists or the agnostics may be. It is self-evident that on this scheme, if it is carried out in all parts of the country, the United States' system of national popular education will be the most efficient and wide instrument for the propagation of atheism which the world has ever seen.[25]

Even in A.A. Hodge's day, he saw the teachings of public education as a devised plan to dismantle absolute truths and indoctrinate children in atheism, relativism and evolutionism. He saw how the public educators were determining and defining the moral fabric for students and the consequences that followed.

In schools today, sex education is a perfect example of this. A moral issue that should be left for the parents to discuss with their child has been deemed an acceptable and necessary school initiative. The *New York Times* ran a piece titled "Does Sex Ed Undermine Parental Rights?" It referenced how the New York City school's chancellor mandated sex-education classes not only exposes young children to graphic sexual acts, but also encourages students to disregard what their parents have taught them at home.[26] This sexual revolution is actually coming from NEA. According to the NEA, students need to be taught more graphic sex-education along with the homosexual lifestyle.[27]

Recently, the New York City Department of Education issued a new mandate requiring *Reducing the Risk* curriculum be taught as a semester course for 6th thru 10th grades. Planned Parenthood endorsed the sex education curriculum, along with Advocates for Youth and the Sexuality Information and Education Council of the United States (SIECUS). The CitizenLink reports, "*Reducing the Risk* gives assignments to students like finding lubricated condoms in drug stores, locating abortion clinics, learning how to use birth control and becoming proficient at installing condoms on wooden penises. Explicit discussions, diagrams and teachings awaken innocent passions before their time and normalize most any distortion of God's original design for sex."[28]

Whatever the duplicity may be, our young and impressionable students are being taken advantage of because the public system has an agenda and believes it has the supreme authority to do so. This only makes sense when considering that public education reinforces the goal for students to become adults who define their own truth and choose their own standards of right and wrong. If parents paid more attention to not only the *content* of instruction but also the *intent* of the public administration, they would be outraged by the deliberate approaches designed to usurp parental authority. The chart below breaks down the difference between the two paradigms discussed thus far.[29]

	OLD PARADIGM	**NEW PARADIGM**
Beliefs	Based on Bible	Blend of New Age & earth-centered religions
Culture	Western individualism	Global solidarity
Values	Based on the Bible (absolute, unchangeable truth)	Based on human idealism (easy to manipulate)
Morals	Moral boundaries	Sensual freedom
Rights	Personal freedom	Social controls
Economy	Free enterprise	Socialist collective
Government	By the people	By those who control the masses

A Bankrupt Education

Since the bureaucratic takeover, the federal government has successfully accrued insurmountable amounts of debt and higher taxes for our nation. Historical trends show that educational spending is at an all-time high. The Department of Education spends roughly a trillion dollars a year on public elementary and secondary education and various educational programs.[30]

Dennis Prager writes, "According to the U.S. Department of Education's National Center for Education Statistics (2010), the United States spent $10,041 per pupil in its public elementary and secondary schools in 2006–2007. Compare this to 1960–61, when America spent $2,769 per pupil (in constant 2007–2008 dollars)—before the Great Society, the War on Poverty, and the establishment of the Department of Education. Nevertheless, American elementary school and high school graduates know less about everything important, and read and write more poorly, than they did when one-fifth the amount of money was spent on education."[31] In spite of the huge spending on education, the public school system is not producing more Einsteins; instead, they have generated higher taxes and more financial debt.

Obviously, the attempt to improve America's education system has been a colossal failure. The federal government has produced poor standards, which has resulted in poor education. Instead of educating and funding qualified and respectable teachers in the classroom, they have deflated the educational system by downgrading quality and efficiency at the same time. The National Research Council conducted a survey and found that both teachers and students are concerned with overcrowded schools, lack of supervision, low retention rates, poor test results, and high dropout rates.[32] Unfortunately, students are not given the proper time or attention needed in order for them to excel.

Too often, students who are not mainstream fall through the cracks and are left behind in the rubble of this broken system. This is not a successful learning environment, but rather a breeding ground for unrest and an open playing field for dangerous ideologies.

An Unsafe Education

Finally, the environment in public schools is getting more violent by the day. The Department of Education has no real answers in solving this problem. In a study conducted by Indicators of School Crime and Safety Report, the report found there were 1,183,700 reported violent crimes in the 2009-2010 school year compared to the 905,000 violent crimes committed in the streets of America. Overall, the report showed that 74 percent of public schools in America reported having crime on their campuses.[33] So the local schools in America, where we send our children on a daily basis, are more dangerous than the streets of America.

On campuses across the country, roughly 5.7 million public school students say gang activity and drug usage are prevalent. Almost half of high school students currently use addictive substances[34] and 75 percent of teen respondents said those active in abusing drugs and alcohol are more likely to engage in sexual activity.[35] In other key findings, over 86 percent of students say they know a classmate who uses drugs, and 44 percent knows someone who sells them on campus.[36]

When you take into account a system with an overarching naturalistic philosophy, union controlled educators, overcrowded schools, poor standards, and massive amounts of financial ruin, there is explainable reason for the violence occurring in the public schools. The public education is a failed system, and one that continues to deteriorate at the expense of our taxpaying dollars and the minds of our children. Left unfettered by political debate, the Department of Education has successfully taken over more of our constitutional rights. If left in power, it will continue to undermine God's biblical mandate for parents to train up their children, and spin its destructive lies that contradict the Bible.[37] But what do public school experts expect when students embody spiritual corruption and behave violently when all they are doing is acting out what they've been taught to believe — mainly that they are animals?

Restoring Education

There are real Christian solutions to these problems that can and will restore the education system of America. We can begin the process of taking back our children's education and improving our schools by abolishing the Department of Education.[38] We need to stop playing politics with education and spending massive amounts of money with so little results.

We need to put education back into the hands of sovereign states. This will increase teacher and parental interaction and provide more structure and accountability on both ends. By returning control of education to the state and local levels it will afford parents a more direct involvement in their child's education (both at home and in their community).[39] Moreover, it will also provide more opportunities and freedom for parents to homeschool their children without certain regulations and compulsory means.

According to the Heritage Foundation research, "Children with involved parents have higher academic achievement. Not only do students score higher on tests but they are more prepared to start school and have a greater likelihood of graduating."[40] Hopefully, this will eliminate the need for teachers unions and the bureaucratic agencies, like NEA and AFA. Listed in the chart below is the difference between state controlled education and federal controlled education.

STATE CONTROL	FED CONTROL
Better Teachers	More Teachers
Better Parental Involvement	More Teacher Unions
Better Church Programs	More Afterschool Programs
Better Coaching	More Standardized Tests
Better Voucher System	More Gov't Money
Better Control From Teachers/Parents	More Control From Gov't

Teachers should not be given tenure without adequate accountability for job performance. One way to do this is to submit before the local school councils a standardized school evaluation approved by educators and parents alike. Could you imagine what would happen if parents were given the power to rate and grade teachers and the administration on a yearly basis? Likewise, families should be able to evaluate and decide if their child is receiving a good and moral education.

Finally, each individual state needs the freedom to develop a voucher system that will better fund the schools in their communities. This chapter only highlighted the threat and offered workable solutions in restoring education. I encourage you to take the time and dig deeper into the public education with the resources I provided in the endnotes.[41]

CHAPTER 8

Threat #2: Redefine Value of Life

"Yet you desired faithfulness even in the womb;
You taught me wisdom in that secret place."
King David

Human life has been boiled down to three controversial words: life, conception and choice. The raging war of ideas going on in America has fostered a growing number of people setting their own societal norms and deciding the value of life. Unlimited autonomy has trounced the belief of life at conception, and the power of choice has become the right of every individual. These philosophies were the driving force behind the 1973 U.S. Supreme Court decision (*Roe v. Wade*) that marked the sanction of abortion in America. Realizing the impact abortion has had on millions and how hotly contested it is morally, politically, and socially in America, let us examine the facts of it with thoughtfulness and objectivity. I believe a common sense approach to the deadly idea of abortion will allow for thought-provoking responses that are sure to be applicable to those lost in this raging war for truth.

Abortion: "It's a choice."

The gruesome nature of abortion has created much turmoil among Americans, particularly Christians. It is a polarizing issue leaving few people on the fence. That aside, we have a young generation of Americans whose worldview is being framed by cultural relativism, who haven't been educated in the real truth about abortion. Many of my students (evangelical Christians) express immediate disapproval of abortion, but are unable to articulate why. This is a matter of life and death because (if left unchallenged) the horrific outcomes of abortion will expand and the death toll will skyrocket to levels never seen in our history.[1]

There is a tremendous need to dialogue with this generation on a level that speaks to them and gives them accurate understanding of abortion. If we do not meet them where they are, we will have an entire generation that will utterly fail to comprehend the moral and social dangers of abortion. It is my prayer that this approach to abortion will help us better understand its deadly threat, and motivate us to engage our culture with the truth.

Life Begins At Conception

It is a medical fact that life begins at conception.[2] If that is true (and it is), it means abortion is the killing of innocent life. And the national tragedy is that America has legalized the killing of innocent life. Since the legalization of abortion in 1973, America has aborted over 50 million babies. That is over 1.2 million babies a year, which if broken down even further is 3,000 abortions every day, or two every minute.[3]

Abortionists avoid the medical facts of life and abortion, and make the *right to choose* a more powerful argument than the *right to life*. They serve up sophisticated marketing campaigns (with slogans like, "Freedom to Choose;" "Keep Your Laws Off My Body;" "Every Child A Wanted Child") designed to sound empowering to women. But the truth remains: a human life is more valuable than the valued commodity of "choice." We need to drive the discussion back to this every time. It is not whether or not a person has the right to choose what is best for them, but that he or she is morally obligated to preserve life given the irrefutable scientific fact that life begins at conception.

A leading philosopher in the debate for abortion, Peter Singer, concedes to this biological fact, "It is possible to give 'human being' a precise meaning. We can use it as equivalent to 'member of the species Homo sapiens'. Whether a being is a member of a given species is something that can be determined scientifically, by an examination of the nature of the chromosomes in the cells of living organisms. In this sense there is no doubt that from the first moments of its existence an embryo conceived from human sperm and eggs is a human being."[4] In an article posted on the Mayo Clinic's website, *Pregnancy Week By Week*, it states, "The zygote has 46 chromosomes – 23 from you and 23 from your partner. These chromosomes will help determine your baby's sex, traits such as eye and hair color, and, to some extent, personality and intelligence."[5] Thus, the zygote (a fertilized ovum) has all the necessary genetic information it needs right from the start.

Furthermore, the theology of the Bible teaches the baby in the mother's womb is indeed human life. The image of God is stamped on every individual, male and female, at the moment of conception (Gen. 1:27). There is a wonderful passage that sheds light into the functionality and awareness of unborn babies in the womb. In Luke 1:44, it reads, "the baby in my womb leaped for joy." The Greek word for baby is *brephos*, and means "a fetus or infant," which is the same Greek word used of a baby after it is born into the world (Lk. 2:12, 16; 18:15). Thus, the Bible is clear that the life in the womb is the same as life out of the womb.

Let's apply some basic logic to the product of birth. If dogs beget dogs, and cats beget cats, and horses beget horses, then humans beget...? The obvious answer is *humans*. The law of biogenesis states that every being reproduces after its own kind. Therefore, any unborn baby is 100 percent human. Because of this, any abortion ought to be considered an extreme action because everyone involved — the mother, father, and doctor — know that a human being is growing inside the mother's womb. They know that every single birth, including their own, resulted from a mother giving birth to a human being. Therefore, this notion that terminating a women's pregnancy is justified because she has the right to choose is nothing more than rejecting the undeniable truth that all unborn babies are human. Commenting on the abortion issue, former President Ronald Reagan remarked, "I've noticed that everybody that is for abortion has already been born."

An unborn baby is not only a human being it is also a human *person*. A person is simply defined as a "living being that has the essential capacity for rational thought, emotional expression, willful direction, and moral reflection concerning him/herself and the world around him/her."[6]

The S.H.A.P.E of an Unborn Baby

The only difference between an unborn baby and a newborn is their S.H.A.P.E. Below is an original acrostic:

> *Size.* A larger human is no more of a person than a smaller one. We wouldn't dismiss a two-year old toddler from being any less human than a thirty-five year old adult. We all began as a tiny zygote, which is of no less value than we are now.
>
> *Habitation.* A person's relative distance from the birth canal is not what distinguishes being "partially" human and "fully" human. We were all conceived in our mother's womb, and we were of no less value than we are now.

Abilities. The inability or lack of ability of an unborn baby to do certain things does not disqualify it as being less human, but simply means it is developing the capacity to do what human persons do. As once a post-natal child who grew and developed certain abilities, we were not any less human than we are now.

Properties. The sperm from the father and the egg from the mother fertilize into a separate entity with 23 chromosomes from dad and 23 chromosomes from mom. All the genetic information necessary to be a human being is comprised in the zygote. The unborn baby has the properties to function as a person; it just doesn't have the current capacity to exercise certain natural properties since it is in the elementary stages of development. This was true for us at conception, but again, didn't mean we were any less human than we are now.

Essentials. An unborn baby needs the same essentials to live as any other human person. The unborn baby needs oxygen, feeding nutrients, and an environment to thrive in order to survive. We were all born because we had these essentials, and we are still in need of them today. Just because unborn babies are dependent on the placenta, uterus and umbilical cord to survive, doesn't mean that they are any less human than we are now.

All unborn babies, who are indeed human persons, should have rights that are protected under the U.S. Constitution. Both the Fifth and Fourteenth Amendments state, "No *person* shall...be deprived of life, liberty, or property, without due process of law." These rights are transcendent rights because they come from God, not government. Thus, every abortion strips the unborn baby (a human person) of its God-given right to be given the right to choose life. This is not only unconstitutional, but it is unfounded, unwarranted, and immoral.

Most research reveals women seek an abortion for economic, emotional and social reasons. It is tragic how many well-meaning women decide irrationally to abort their unborn baby because of their circumstances. Though we can be sympathetic to the hardships many women face, an unborn child should not be considered a problem to be disposed of. Choosing to avoid consequences does not compare to the horrific decision of taking an innocent life. The responsibility of a new baby may result in financial difficulty, require educational pursuits be put on hold, and impede some personal relationships, but there are solutions beyond taking the life of the unborn.

Women contemplating abortion should be encouraged to consider adoption. There are thousands of couples on waiting lists eagerly waiting to adopt a baby. These adoptive parents are prepared to bear the financial and economic demands of raising a child, are emotionally committed to loving and nurturing that child within the confines of their family, and welcome the difference a new baby would bring to their social status. Pregnancy is not meant to be a punishment, but a blessing from God. Therefore, *economic, emotional* and *social* reasons for abortion can be overcome.

Steve Wagner offers what he calls *Outline of the One-Minute Pro-life Apologist*. This is a great outline to follow when you find yourself in a position where you need to layout a simple argument in favor of pro-life in only a minute.

1. The unborn is a human being.
2. Born or unborn, all of us need only a proper environment and adequate nutrition.
3. There is one equal quality among all valuable human beings: human nature
4. To vindicate women's rights we must base our case on human nature.
5. If human nature is the valuable thing about women, and the unborn has it, we should protect the unborn just like we protect women.[7]

Ending Abortion

So far I've provided a common sense approach to abortion that can be readily used in day-to-day conversations with people. I urge each Christian to take the information in this book and spread the truth about abortion to as many people and places as they can. We can win this battle against abortion if churches decide to address it head on and educate their congregations to stop sitting idly by as thousands of unborn babies are murdered in America everyday.[8]

We would think with all the petitioning, lobbying, praying, and rallying against abortion, it would have been overturned by now. But it hasn't. Why? The reason is because most people aren't concerned about it. They are not concerned because they don't know the truth about abortion. Most Americans believe that murder is morally wrong. That's why we need to accurately inform people in our churches, in our schools, and in our communities, that life begins at conception, and therefore abortion is the murder of innocent life.

Ray Comfort produced a short documentary called "180" that parallels the atrocities of Hitler and the holocaust to that of abortion in America.[9] I encourage readers to watch this film and show it to as many people as possible. It will provide insight into what people think about abortion along with great questions to ask regarding their belief in morals and the value of life. This is extremely helpful because the average American finds the controversial abortion issue tricky at best. Comparing abortion to the holocaust immediately sets the tone and proper context of the conversation. This approach allows people to correctly view the unborn baby as a human person, leading them to conclude that abortion is no different than the mass murder of millions at the hands of Hitler. It also reveals the falsity of arguments that include a difficult situation, an unexpected pregnancy, or simply a woman's choice can excuse the taking of innocent life, and that clearly, it is morally wrong.

If people view abortion within this framework, we can shift much of America back to pro-life. R.C. Sproul's book, *Abortion: A Rational Look at an Emotional Issue*, puts the abortion into historical context: "Resistance to unjust laws and dehumanizing practices may be costly...the world still recoils in horror at the reality of the Holocaust in Nazi Germany. Yet I believe we are in the midst of a new and more evil holocaust, which sees the destruction of 1.5 million unborn babies every year in the United States alone."[10]

On the ending of abortion, the great preacher and author, John Piper, writes:

> It was right for William Wilberforce to devote twenty years of his life in Parliament to the abolition of English slave trading, even though the great majority of those merchants who gave up the trade did it under constraint and not for any holy reasons at all. It was the work of God's grace that rid England of the barbarisms of the African slave trade. And therefore the Lord looked down with delight on February 22, 1807, when the House of

Commons passed the decisive bill. The same will be true when persevering pro-life forces bring an end to wanton, legalized child-killing in America. . . .My prayer is that the truth of God's pleasure in public justice will inspire many in our day to take up the mantle of William Wilberforce and wear it into battle against the manifold injustices of our day.[11]

If Christians want to see Roe v. Wade overturned, then we need to build an infrastructure that is tied to as many churches, businesses, organizations, lobbyists, judges, and local and state legislatures as possible. We must strategically coordinate our efforts and not deter from our mission until we see abortion banned for good in America. Start now by staying informed and educate your family on abortion.[12] Be active in volunteering or starting a pro-life group in your church. Get your family and church involved in organizing a "Walk For Life" to help fund and support clinics that provide free ultrasounds, medical treatment, counseling, and financial support to unwed mothers. Be sure to only vote for candidates that are pro-life and have plans to implement legislation that opposes abortion and defunding of Planned Parenthood.

As a follower of Jesus Christ and a preacher of grace, there is forgiveness for anyone who has supported, advocated, performed, and followed through with an abortion. A beautiful Psalm of David expresses: "When we were overwhelmed by sins, you forgave our transgressions (Ps. 65:3)." Elsewhere David prayed, "You, Lord, are forgiving and good, abounding in love to all who call to you (Ps. 86:5)." Though abortion is a grievous act and morally reprehensible to God, His mercy and forgiveness is greater. God's love is too great to pass up, and it is available to all who turn to Him in repentance. Furthermore, each aborted and unwanted baby is in the loving arms of God in heaven (2 Sam. 12:23). I pray this brings comfort and healing to the many who are wounded and scarred by the guilt and regret brought on by abortion.

CHAPTER 9

Threat #3: Replace Traditional Marriage

"What God has joined together, let no one separate."
Mark 10:9

Homosexuality, no doubt, has become a power-driven topic that is finding its way into every level of our society. Whether it is through legislation or indoctrination on school campuses, homosexuality is gaining more ground than ever before. Many gay activists have been working tirelessly for years to convince the younger generation to endorse their lifestyle and political agendas. In 1989, gay activists outlined a revolution in a book titled, *After the Ball: How America Will Conquer Its Fears and Hatred of Gays in the 90s*. In the book, Marshall Kirk and Hunter Madsen lay out a systematic approach in taking over the media and education system in efforts to persuade the public to accept their lifestyle. The striking point is that they have succeeded in accomplishing almost everything they set out to do back in the 1980s.

Homosexuality: "We're the new normal."

Homosexuality is currently being exploited in every avenue of the media. What once was taboo and unspeakable has now become the norm for every family sit-com and primetime television show. Turning on the television any given night will yield a number of different shows that not only portray the normality of the gay lifestyle, but even make it appealing and comedic. There is an agenda behind this: accept homosexuality as the norm.

By weighing so favorably with the media (the media being one of its biggest proponents), the Gay Agenda has made significant inroads among young people and has played a huge role in shaping their beliefs and values in support of the homosexual lifestyle. Completely unprecedented, we are seeing many young people shifting sides and now advocating for the right for same-sex couples to marry and enjoy the same entitlements of heterosexual couples. In 2008, Pew Forum conducted a poll of 18-29 year olds and found that over 50 percent of them supported same-sex "marriage." That may not come as a surprise, but these 18-29 year olds surveyed classified themselves as evangelical Christians. That's right; over half of young supposed evangelicals support same-sex "marriage."

With this growing network, it will not be long until a whole new generation of homosexuals and supporters will be triumphant in legalizing same-sex "marriage" in America. Should this occur, the traditional family structure will undergo a radical alteration in the cultural and traditional mindset. Fortunately, in response to the Gay Agenda, a majority of states have passed amendments to their state constitutions that protect traditional marriage by defining marriage strictly as the union of one man and one woman. Though the institution of marriage is essential to our existence, it is now being questioned, challenged, and, in some cases, redefined (as though it could be!). Homosexuals will not stop their campaign until same-sex "marriage" is legalized in every state across America. Let's take a closer look at how the homosexual lobby is changing the mind of our youth.

The Gay Agenda

First, homosexual activists paint traditionalists to be bigots and religious fanatics who hate homosexuals with a passion. Second, they have the cultural media at their disposal, and they exercise this power to advance their moral agenda. Third, they argue that homosexual love relationships are no different than heterosexual love relationships. Fourth, they fund lobbyists who will get them exactly what they want, both politically and corporately. Fifth, they've gained enormous support from major corporations that have provided financial backing, political prowess, and educational awareness and training (e.g., Home Depot, Pepsi-Cola, Apple, and Target, to name only a few). Sixth, they have infiltrated the school systems and argued for more rights for gay teachers to publicly announce their lifestyle in the classroom. Seventh, they have the backing of the majority of Hollywood as increasingly more TV shows and films portray the gay lifestyle as commonplace, fun, invigorating, and most importantly, acceptable. Indeed, while same-sex "marriage" may not be fully embraced in our society, it certainly is on TV!

Tolerating Diversity

To gain a better understanding of the Gay Agenda and how it is being used to advance its ideals in our society, let's take a look at five key categories that homosexual activists have intentionally devised or capitalized on in efforts to "normalize" the homosexual lifestyle within the culture:

1. *"Out of the closet" friends*—One factor that has changed the opinion of so many youth today is, quite simply, how many gay friends they have. Gay activists provide a strong network to rally as many

confused and struggling individuals as possible, and then promote the acceptance of their "alternative" sexual lifestyle by branding friends that don't accept their behavior as homophobic. Further, gay activists promote the idea that experimenting with homosexuality is a natural and healthy expression of sexuality. Teens are already vulnerable to the pressures of sex, and this is a new vista being presented. They are inundated with lies including the well-worn and effective "everyone is doing it, so why shouldn't they."

2. *Media saturation* — As mentioned prior, our youth are constantly bombarded by the lies and propaganda of homosexuality on TV, on the Internet, in movies, in campaigns and celebrity lifestyles, in magazines, in sex education, and in books on the topic. Every time they turn on the TV, they see nothing but immoral behavior and a dysfunctional version of the family. They don't see families embracing wholesome values that provide a great deal of support. Aided by the media, the true normal and natural (i.e., heterosexuality and traditional marriage) is tainted or removed completely, making it painlessly easy for viewers to swallow a new normal — homosexuality and same-sex "marriage."

3. *Church reluctance* — Instead of the church dealing with homosexuality head on from the pulpit, it has chosen to hide behind it. Gay activists have worked extremely hard to remove churches from the debate surrounding society's acceptance of the homosexual lifestyle. Not only have their efforts been successful in the promotion of the Gay Agenda, but unfortunately, most churches have retreated so far from the debate that they have even neglected their responsibility to reach out to homosexuals with

the love of God. Thus, the Gay Agenda marches on unquestioned by a vast majority of churches, and homosexuals remain confused and trapped in their destructive lifestyle.

4. *Tongue-tied beliefs*—I have conducted many seminars and classes on the topic of homosexuality and have found that far too many students get tongue-tied when confronted with their friends' homosexuality. The common response from a young evangelical is, "I know the Bible condemns it, but I still think people should have the right to love who they want to." Or, "God wants us to love others. It's not up to me to judge." How is it that we are in a day and age when homosexuals are now the ones educating evangelicals on what God *really* thinks about homosexuality? Shouldn't it be the other way around?

5. *Hypocrisy*—Our youth have seen, read and heard about leaders condemning the homosexual lifestyle while secretly indulging in its very lusts! Gay activists love to point out hypocrisy. Taking the focus off of their lifestyle and portraying the injustice of others–garnering the sympathy of others. This has played well to their favor because hypocrisy and intolerance is a huge turn-off to teens and twenty-somethings.

These are just a few of the plays in the Gay Agenda playbook that have been used to brainwash young people into believing that any and all relationships are normal and appropriate on all accounts. They use tactics such as **moral relativism** (*Homosexuality is my truth*); **tolerance** (*Homosexuality must be accepted by all*); and **normalization** (*Homosexuality is normal*). Every time a homosexual makes the tolerance plea it pushes young people further into believing that homosexuality is decent and right.

Homosexuals target our youth because they know that if the youth buy into their agenda, they will willingly usher in the next phase of indoctrination for the next generation and so on. For instance, have you noticed that the Gay Agenda has crept into sex education in Kindergarten classrooms? Do you think it's because it will help our kids develop into bright and talented Americans? No! It is designed to steal the innocence from our children by exposing them to immoral acts. I find this to be no different than child pornography and wonder why this isn't considered a crime.[1]

The Gay Agenda Exposed

Specifically, who are the groups targeting our youth? They are the GLSEN (Gay, Lesbian and Straight Education Network), HRC (Human Rights Campaign), GLAAD (Gay & Lesbian Alliance Against Defamation), GSA Network (Gay-Straight Alliance), Human Rights Campaign, and NGLTF (National Gay and Lesbian Task Force). All of these organizations have one thing in common: *change America by normalizing the homosexual lifestyle*. All of these groups have strong political ties with major networks from Hollywood to Washington. They are getting more votes, amassing more funds, and legislating more and more of their homosexual lifestyle across the nation.

The next time homosexuals have a Gay Pride Parade, take a look at how young the majority of the participants are in attendance. It is beyond troubling to see that the Gay Agenda has completely captivated an entire culture of young people into believing that a perverse sexual lifestyle should be accepted as normal. To see so many of them fighting for a cause they really know nothing about is heartbreaking.

I have counseled many young people who found themselves caught in this destructive behavior, and witnessed the pain and betrayal parents have felt when their children have told them they are gay. Even in my limited experience in counseling families with issues related to homosexuality, the support network within the church is strikingly deficient compared to the support system provided by the Gay Agenda. Day after day our youth are bombarded by the cultural media that funds, endorses and celebrates homosexuality, while our churches, meanwhile, offer paltry sermons on the topic and little, if any, support for those struggling with these issues.

In her book, *The Death of Right and Wrong,* Tammy Bruce (an open lesbian) explains that in her early years as a feminist, she was very active in advancing the Gay Agenda. She tells how she spent long hours and many days using mass media to brainwash the public into believing that homosexuality isn't about sexual practices, but merely an "alternative lifestyle."[2] I appreciate Bruce's honesty concerning the tactics of the Gay Agenda, but that kind of information reveals a very scary reality: there is an army of homosexual activists who are propagating their doctrine to the vulnerable minds of our youth for their own sexual gain. Their agenda has nothing to do with protecting the rights of humanity; it has to do with performing their sexual desires with acceptance and acclamation without regard to moral truth.

Taken straight from the GLSEN website, their mission is as follows:

> The Gay, Lesbian & Straight Education Network strives to assure that each member of every school community is valued and respected regardless of sexual orientation or gender identity/expression. We believe that such an atmosphere engenders a positive sense of self, which is the basis of educational achievement and personal growth.

Since homophobia and heterosexism undermine a healthy school climate, we work to
educate teachers, students and the public at
large about the damaging effects these forces
have on youth and adults alike. We recognize that forces such as racism and sexism
have similarly adverse impacts on communities and we support schools in seeking to
redress all such inequities. GLSEN seeks to
develop school climates where difference is
valued for the positive contribution it makes
in creating a more vibrant and diverse community. We welcome as members any and all
individuals, regardless of sexual orientation,
gender identity/expression or occupation,
who are committed to seeing this philosophy
realized in K-12 schools.[3]

I think it would be advantageous if we ask ourselves a
few thought-provoking questions before moving on. First,
what on earth does GLSEN mean when they say that they
"strive to assure" that our schools respect and value "sexual
orientation or gender identity/expression?" Who fits under
this ambiguous definition of "sexual orientation" and
"gender identity expression?" I have done a little research
and found that it includes, but is not limited to: lesbians, gay
men, transgendered persons, transsexuals, transvestites,
bi-sexuals, cross dressers, pansexuals, and polysexuals. So
my question is, what is stopping someone from adding a
pedophile or sadomasochist to this list? GLSEN states that
they "welcome any and all individuals, regardless of sexual
orientation," so we must assume that a pedophile would fit
into this description. The truth is, when GLSEN walks on to
your kid's school campus to educate them on "sexual orientation" or "gender identity" it's all a ploy to get them to

support bisexuality, cross dressers, pansexuals, polysexuals, and homosexuals! And remember, they call that education, and they are getting away with it!

Second, "gender identity expressions" is more than just educating our students about *tolerance*. It is about conforming their minds to embrace a destructive homosexual lifestyle that paves the way for acceptance of any kind of sexual deviation. It has worked to their advantage to lump every sexual lifestyle together to convince schools across America that these "gender identity expressions" are normal and good for society.

Third, GLSEN believes the true meaning and purpose of education should be a "positive sense of self, which is the basis of educational achievement and personal growth." In a 2002 report, GLSEN states that: "Despite those who would like education to focus solely on scholastic aptitude, schools have always been places where societal values are transmitted and prejudices of all kinds routinely addressed. Where heterosexism causes uneven social and learning opportunities — and it does everywhere — it stands to reason that schools would want to squarely face the issue and level this imbalance."

Translation? By advancing sexual desires and altering the way our youth think about the sexual makeup of heterosexuals we will help give our youth a positive self-image. Obviously this will not achieve personal growth for our youth and is simply a ploy for the Gay Agenda to achieve their own personal growth in schools, and eventually have power to control our children. It is only a matter of time before America's educational system will be filled with administrators and teachers who are actively and openly practicing their unorthodox lifestyle and calling it "freedom of expression through sexual orientation."

Fourth, what exactly is GLSEN teaching our teachers and students? Ironically, parents are often the last to know what their children are being taught, especially when it comes to sexuality. It is not until their child comes home with a book entitled, "Everybody Has Those Thoughts: So It Doesn't Mean You're Gay," that they learn what is being taught. GLSEN also sponsors "The Day of Silence" once a year on school campuses as an expression of students' support of the Gay Agenda in public schools. But that's not all. In 2009, the California Assembly passed a bill establishing the Harvey Milk Day for public schools. Harvey Milk was the first openly gay man elected to public office in California. This is just another angle perpetrated by GLSEN to proselytize students about homosexuality while in school. But one has to wonder if GLSEN says it is teaching "societal values" to our children, why aren't parents able to vote on the material and gay-pride days before they are issued on schools campuses?[4]

Fifth, GLSEN uses the word "heterosexism" as a way to say that being heterosexual is somehow arrogant or wrong. Even so, I wonder how GLSEN is striving to assure that they are providing the same due diligence for those couples who are in heterosexual relationships, as they are for homosexual ones? There is continuous talk about tolerance, and yet GLSEN doesn't have any tolerance for what Christians have to say on this matter. Christians argue for traditional marriage (which is the bedrock for all civilization), while homosexuals argue for diversified sexual relationships (which will devastate all civilization).

Sixth, GLSEN states that it seeks to create a more "vibrant and diverse community," so I have to wonder if that includes the identity/expression of Christians who believe marriage is between a man and a woman? Of course, GLSEN is not intent on creating a "vibrant and diverse community" that consists of traditionalists raising a family they conceived naturally together. If GLSEN wanted to foster a "healthy school climate" then they first ought to be responsible to explain to parents (who have the God-given power over their children) what their agenda truly is.

Seventh, I wonder how the GLSEN organization is lawfully allowed in the school systems in the first place. If they can be given access to teach our children their version of tolerance and acceptance to promote equality, what is to stop other organizations from promoting their agendas? Ironically, after September 11, most pastors were banned from public schools for "security reasons," but agencies like GLSEN were given full access to administrations, teachers, and most importantly, our children. Currently, the Gay Agenda has been successful in their "Day of Action" campaigns, which are large-scale events designed to make a big impression on school campuses and in communities all across America. So far they have GLBT History Month (October), Transgender Day of Remembrance (November), Day of Silence (April), and Harvey Milk Day (May).[5]

Lastly, I must admit that I have real trouble when GLSEN attempts to liken its efforts to the Civil Rights movement of the 1960s. Homosexuality has absolutely nothing in common with color or religion, despite what GLSEN wants you to believe. This is simply the Gay Agenda's attempt to hijack a sensitive issue like civil rights and classify homosexuals as an oppressed class of people. This tactic is very crafty, but the argument is self-defeating: homosexuality is a behavior, and a person's skin has nothing to do with behavior. Importantly, and quite simply, "sexual orientation" is not a suspect classification and is not entitled to the heightened protections afforded to individuals on the basis of race, sex, religion, and the like. The U.S. Supreme Court has been very clear on the types of groups that are entitled to increased protection. For instance, "suspect classes" must exhibit immutable characteristics, be a politically powerless group, and have suffered a history of discrimination. While homosexuals may argue that they have suffered a history of discrimination, they absolutely cannot argue that they exhibit immutable characteristics or are a politically power-less group. And before you ask how religion could possibly be a suspect classification since it is not an immutable char-acteristic, allow me to put your mind at ease: religion does not need this kind of justification to demand special pro-tections for it. All the justification it needs for heightened protection is the First Amendment of the U.S. Constitution. Religious freedom is, after all, our *first* freedom.

David Kupelian wrote a profound article entitled, *Why Conservatives are Abandoning the Gay Issue*. In his article he points out,

> We've progressed *way* beyond free sex. News reports today showcase an epidemic of school teachers having sex with their underage students, teen 'sexting' and ram-pant middle-school 'hookups,' transgenders marching in parades proudly displaying their surgically mutilated bodies, and ever-increasing tolerance of adult-child sex. Perhaps most troubling – at least in terms of its potential to shred the fabric of Judeo-Christian civilization – is so-called 'same-sex marriage.' The God-ordained union of man and woman, the wellbeing of children (who need both father and mother), the soundness of the family as the basic 'cell' of a strong and healthy body politic – all this vanishes when the sacredness of marriage is violated and mocked.[6]

Make no mistake. It is up to traditionalists (who hold to a Judeo-Christian ethic) to make sure that this current gen-eration is equipped with truth that will bring healing to the homosexual community, bring sweeping change against the tide of GLSEN, and stir our national conscience to return to its original values and respect of traditional marriage.

The Fight for a Gay America

In pushing their agenda, the homosexual movement has defined equality to be: *any human being (despite their sex) has the freedom and right to marry whomever they wish.* This view boasts that same-sex couples actually enhance the overall quality and wellbeing of the social family arrangement. They often use their sentimental argument in the form of a question: "What is the harm of a loving same-sex couple?" Furthermore, this thinking believes that each community determines its own set of understanding of language and responsibility, and therefore, the more we embrace the idea that people can *reinterpret* their own way of life, the more advanced that community will become in overcoming religious barriers.

In addition, if same-sex "marriage" is a new construct embraced by people, then that same-sex couple has the right to raise a family; whether it is through foster care, adoption, artificial insemination, or through surrogate mothering. However, this evidence exposes the faulty thinking advocated by homosexuality and clearly demonstrates that deconstructing traditional marriage would be morally threatening to the protection and vitality of our nation. Think about it. If the homosexual worldview was implemented throughout all the systems of life, what would that do to our society? The central purpose of our government is to promote the general welfare of all people by protecting its citizens from any harm that seeks to destroy their way of life. In order for freedom and justice to prevail among the equal rights of each person, the government must do what is best for society's health, security, and long-term viability.

It has already been noted that the Gay Agenda is not only to *deconstruct* traditional marriage, but also to *reconstruct* a social matrimony that will have devastating effects on the livelihood of all Americans!

We see how homosexuality is plastered all over the cultural media with cheapened exploitations, infatuations of unrestricted sex before marriage (without lasting consequences), and not to forget the blatant infidelity of heterosexual and homosexual relations. What this does is marginalize traditional marriage and replace it with an "updated version" that makes the homosexual lifestyle very appealing. Increasingly, TV, movies, advertising, the Internet and news media celebrate homosexuality and portray it as completely normal and as socially acceptable as traditional marriage. At its core, viewers are brainwashed with images designed to infuse a targeted ideology that conforms an entire generation into believing that the homosexual lifestyle is exciting and just as normal as any heterosexual relationship.

Pause and consider that. The cultural media and the Gay Agenda are becoming the dominating influence in this country, with the power and plan to shape the minds and hearts of generations to come. Using all available communication means, gay activists are sending a biased message that undermines the family model and supplies the culture with a lie. They are intent on trading the ideals of faith, family and country for self-centeredness, hedonism and self-absorption.

Parents all across America need to wake up and realize their God-given right and responsibility as the number one influence in the lives of their children. Parents must not abdicate to the cultural media! This is precisely why the family home in America is under such heavy attack: whoever controls the family controls the ideas that set the course for tomorrow. The cost is too great to allow the homosexual dogma of the cultural media to redefine our faith, families, and country. We must endeavor to stand on God's truth and hold to His moral absolutes at all costs.

Comparing Itself to Traditional Marriage

It is vitally important that we fully understand why traditional marriage is the only morally good agent to sustain and enrich family life. At the same time, exposing why same-sex "marriage" is morally threatening to the protection and vitality of the world.

The union between a man and a woman has been considered the normal and healthiest model of marriage for all civilizations. This is based on the Judeo-Christian ethic that the sacredness of marriage is shared between a man and a woman. The philosophy of cultural relativism, on the other hand, vigorously opposes the ethical values of traditional marriage and endorses the new ethics of same-sex "marriage." This worldview is, more or less, supported on three major levels: (1) Homosexuality is a legitimate and normal lifestyle because some people are born gay; (2) It is unjust to discriminate against homosexuals on the premise that they are a threat to society; and (3) If allowed to thrive through the legalization of same-sex "marriage," homosexuality will enhance human development and social progress.[7] Let's examine each particular argument from the homosexual perspective before offering a response.

1. Normalization

In efforts to establish the normalcy of homosexuality, homosexuals often refer to a study done by Alfred Kinsey as scientific evidence that homosexuals are born gay.[8] Furthermore they cite The American Psychological Association (APA), which argues that homosexual orientation is normal. The APA, for example, states "recent evidence suggests that biology, including genetic or inborn hormonal factors, play a significant role in a person's sexuality." They go on to claim that one's own sexual orientation is not a conscious choice that can be voluntarily changed."[9]

2. Discrimination

Homosexuals argue that traditionalism is an intolerant religious worldview that inserts its own biased definition of marriage. By doing this, homosexuals insist that traditionalists are ignoring their natural rights by enforcing their religious values through the restrictions and guidelines of traditional marriage.

An announcement came in May of 2012 from the NAACP, which passed this historic resolution:

> The NAACP Constitution affirmatively states our objective to ensure the 'political, education, social and economic equality' of all people. Therefore, the NAACP has opposed and will continue to oppose any national, state, local policy or legislative initiative that seeks to codify discrimination or hatred into the law or to remove the Constitutional rights of LGBT citizens. We support marriage equality consistent with equal protection under the law provided under the Fourteenth Amendment of the United States Constitution. Further, we strongly affirm the religious freedoms of all people as protected by the First Amendment.[10]

This has been precisely what the Gay Agenda has been advocating for quite some time. To mention an example, in a published issue of *The Advocate* (December, 2008) the cover story read, "Gay is the New Black: The Last Great Civil Rights Struggle." The writer of the article, Michael Gross, wrote, "These past few years we've made so much progress that we'd begun to think everybody saw us as we see ourselves. Suddenly we were faced with the reality that a majority of voters don't like us, don't think we're normal, don't believe our lives and loves count as much or are worth as much as theirs."[11]

That is to say, Michael Gross and the gay community affirm they and their partners who are committed to one another should not be restricted from marrying one another. Therefore, they avow that homosexuals ought to be given the right to marry their partner, and not be denied their constitutional rights or discriminated from their equal civil marriage rights.

3. Enhancement

The final argument from homosexuals is the improvement of marital and family development provided by same-sex "marriage." In point of fact, David Noebel summarizes their reasoning in these words, "The concepts of biological and cultural evolution dictate that the traditional concepts of marriage and family have outlived their usefulness. As the human species and culture progress, old traditions become outdated and must be replaced by new concepts that will continue the evolutionary process."[12] Basically, homosexuality is premised on the belief that if same-sex couples were allowed to marry, they would provide greater stability and security to their families.

Homosexuals point out that more studies are revealing there is not a single difference in developmental areas such as intelligence, psychological, social, and popularity among classmates from children who are raised by homosexual parents.[13] They argue that they should be given the right to practice their sexuality openly by marrying whomever they wish and raising as many children as they wish, whether through foster care, adoption, artificial insemination, or surrogate mothering.

A response to the arguments presented by the Gay Agenda will demonstrate a consistent defense to a Judeo-Christian ethic, while showing the natural benefits that come from traditional marriage logically follow, and anything that seeks to replace or add to it would be morally wrong for civilization.

Response #1 – It's not about being normal it's about the truth

Homosexuals are wrong in stating that they are born with a "gay gene." There is no scientific evidence to support that a person is born gay. In other words, the "gay gene" theory is just that—theory, not fact.[14]

Assuming there was a gay-gene, how is it passed on if homosexuals are unable to reproduce? Or take twins for example. How is the gay gene theory justified if one twin is gay and the other one isn't? Considering that identical twins have identical genes, there should be a concordance rate of 100 percent whenever one twin is homosexual, the other should be as well. However, that is simply not what we find when put to the test.[15]

Let's assume for the sake of argument that homosexuals are, in fact, born gay. If that were the case, then that line of reasoning would also apply to pedophiles, rapists, and drug addicts. Norman Geisler rightly says, "Even if there were an inherited tendency toward a homosexual attitude, this would not justify homosexual acts. Some people seem to inherit a tendency toward violence, but this does not justify violent acts. Some people are said to have an inherited tendency toward alcohol abuse, but this does not justify drunkenness."[16] Thus, being born gay wouldn't automatically normalize the behavior or make it morally right. Furthermore, even if there were a "gay-gene" it wouldn't be *normal*; it would indicate a genetic *mutation*. According to the principles of natural selection, the "gay gene" would be considered a biological mistake because homosexuals can't procreate and don't create the best environment for the family.

The National Association for Research and Therapy of Homosexuality (NARTH) released the results of a two-year study that concluded that homosexuals could change his or her sexual orientation.[17] But if homosexuals are born gay, how do we explain the countless homosexuals who sought help, got treatment, and stopped living a homosexual lifestyle? The answer is simple: *Life didn't choose certain people to be gay; certain people chose to be gay in life*. Evidence points to the fact that homosexuality is an individual choice, not a choice made by nature or God.

Response #2 – It's about protecting human rights not human choices

There is absolutely no discrimination in claiming that a homosexual does not have the right to marry. In fact, the person who chooses to be homosexual does have the same privileges and benefits of state-sanctioned matrimony. They, like their heterosexual counterparts, simply cannot marry a person of the same-sex. This is the legal disconnect among homosexuals that needs to be understood. It is not a matter of being denied the right to marriage, but more a matter of denied the right to redefine marriage according to their sexual preferences. Greg Koukl addresses the issue as follows:

Gay Citizens already have the same right to

marry as anyone else—subject to the same restrictions. No one may marry a close blood relative, a child, a person who is already married, or a person of the same-sex. However, much of these restrictions may disappoint the incestuous, pedophiles, polygamists, and homosexuals, the issue is not discrimination. It is the nature of marriage itself.[18]

The fact remains, homosexuals choose not to recognize that marriage has always been between a man and a woman, and has been the basic foundation of humanity. Greg Koukl further writes, "The truth is, it is not culture that constructs marriages or the families that marriages begin. Rather, it is the other way around: Marriage and family construct culture. As the building blocks of civilization, families are logically prior to society as the parts are prior to the whole."[19] Koukl is right. The sociological perspective on traditional marriage reveals a stronger and healthier society, and if tampered with, causes severe problems to the society as a whole.[20]

Furthermore, homosexuals are wrong to equate same-sex "marriage" with traditional marriage because it is not equal anatomically, does not have the natural design to procreate, and cannot offer the diversity of a father/mother role in parenting children through life. There is a natural complement between the husband and wife. Males express their masculinity, while females express their femininity. Homosexual couples do not have this natural teleology. Hence, it is not legally or morally permissible to redefine marriage for the sole purpose of promoting sexual predilections, but is a moral obligation to reaffirm traditional marriage. There are standards by which the state issues marriage licenses and it is regulated by how they meet these fundamental standards.

Still, homosexuals feel strongly that the government is

responsible for legislating their predisposition to same-sex "marriage" and provide them social and political respect from the rest of society. The real issue is that homosexuals want people to believe that their constitutional rights are being infringed upon, when in reality, they are infringing their views on those who support societal norms. Furthermore, homosexuals misinterpret the U.S. Constitution every time they invoke it. The U.S. Constitution is a founding document that protects and affirms the human rights of citizens of the United States, not the particular sexual orientation citizens choose to live out. Therefore, to legalize same-sex "marriage" is not a matter of *affirming* human *rights*, but rather, it is a matter of *validating* human *choices*. That is not the kind of business the government is permitted to do under the Bill of Rights.

Response #3 – It won't make things better it will only make it worse

Given the fact that same-sex "marriage" has no logical leg to stand on; it also possesses no real moral improvement to society. Tim Leslie says it well: "If the central purpose of government is to promote the general welfare, then the state must promote always what is best for society's health, security, and long term viability.[21] If the government were to legalize same-sex "marriage," it does more than just permit two people of the same-sex to get married. The government would be adopting a worldview lifestyle that would corrupt the very fabric of moral living in our society. Dr. Voddie Baucham writes, "Perhaps the most damning aspect of the civil rights argument is logical unsustainability. If sexual orientation/identity is the basis for (1) classification as a minority group, and (2) legal grounds for the redefinition of marriage, then what's to stop the "bisexual" from fighting for the ability to marry a man and a woman simultaneously since his "orientation" is, by definition, directed toward both sexes? What about the member of NAMBLA whose orientation is toward young boys? Where do we stop, and on what basis? Homosexual advocates are loath to answer this question."[22]

Therefore, to oppose same-sex "marriage" as well as correct its destructive behavior is not synonymous with discrimination or bigotry. Traditional marriage is not a matter of *preference*, but a matter of *reference* to the foundation of human social order. So when we oppose same-sex "marriage," we are basing it on facts that show traditional marriage as the natural superstructure that provides the most enriching benefits not only for the family unit but for the rest of society as well. Interestingly, studies on same-sex couples in Norway, Canada, Sweden, Netherlands, Belgium, Portugal, Spain and other places (as well)[23] are beginning to reveal that homosexuality is actually very destructive to the couple and society as a whole.

Below is a concise, yet thorough, review of some of the issues that highlight the physical and moral decay within the homosexual community. The implication of these facts clearly and objectively demonstrates that homosexuality stands to destroy the moral bedrock of civilization along with many of the lives caught in this sexual behavior.

1. ***Promiscuity.*** In his book *Straight and Narrow?* Dr. Thomas Schmidt shows that over 75 percent of homosexual men have over 100 sexual partners in their lifetime.[24] In Alan Bell and Martin Weinberg's book *Homosexualities*, they discovered that 28 percent of male homosexuals had more than 1,000 partners, and over 79 percent admitted that more than half of their sexual encounters were with total strangers.[25] In the *Advocate* (a homosexual magazine), a report found that 20 percent of homosexuals admitted to

having anywhere from 51-300 sexual partners in their lifetime, and approximately another 8 percent having had more than 300 sexual partners.[26]

2. *Sexual Diseases.* Sexually transmitted diseases and AIDS run rampant among homosexuals. 75 percent of homosexual men carry one or more sexually transmitted diseases (gonorrhea, bacterial infections and syphilis). In addition, over 65 percent have viral infections like herpes and hepatitis B.[27] At the 2010 STD Prevention Conference sponsored by the Center for Disease Control and Prevention, statistics revealed that the rate of new HIV diagnoses among men who have sex with men is more than forty-four times that of other men and more than forty times that of women.[28] According to the Gay and Lesbian Medical Association, lesbians have the highest risk for breast cancer and cervical cancer.[29]

3. *Life Expectancy.* Dr. Paul Cameron (psychologist and sex researcher) along with his researched team revealed alarming statistics of the life expectancy among homosexuals. His compiled data reported the median age of lesbian is 45 years old and the median age of gay men to be 42 years old. For gay men with AIDS it is 39 years old.[30] When compared to the average life expectancy of married heterosexual men, the difference in life expectancy is almost 35 years.[31]

4. *Proselytizing Children.* Kerby Anderson (President of Probe Ministries) reports that GLSEN is entering our school systems to teach our children that it is healthy and beneficial for children to begin experimenting sexually at a young age. He states that GLSEN wants children to know it is perfectly normal for children to express their interest in homosexuality and that it is appropriate and even

necessary for children to interact with older homosexuals and learn about the normalcy of their lifestyle.[32] However, not only is the Gay Agenda seeking to proselytize children with homosexuality, but advocating for more pedophilia relationships as well (The Journal of Homosexuality, International Lesbian and Gay Association, and North American Man/Boy Love Association). For example, an article by Dr. Brongersma stated that parents should not view a pedophile "as a rival or competitor, not as a thief of their property, but as a partner in the boy's upbringing, someone to be welcomed into their home..."[33]

5. *Mental Problems.* Dr. William Lane Craig notes in his book that homosexuals are three times more likely to become alcoholics. This explains why over half of the gay community has a history of drug and alcohol abuse.[34] According to Dr. Schmidt, 40 percent of homosexual men struggle with depression, while 37 percent of female homosexuals have a history of depression.[35] Findings from the *New Family Structures Study* revealed higher social, emotional and relational problems from adult children (18-39) raised by same-sex parents than adult children who were raised by heterosexual couples.[36] In a population-based study of young people conducted in New Zealand (2005), the research found that homosexuality is ". . . associated with increasing rates of depression, anxiety, illicit drug dependence, suicidal thoughts and attempts." Gay males, the study shows, have mental health problems five times higher than young heterosexual males. Lesbians have mental health problems nearly twice those of exclusively heterosexual females.[37]

6. *Family Deterioration.* Most research shows that

homosexuals do not remain in a monogamous relationship.[38] Furthermore, children raised by same-sex couples are less likely to conform to traditional gender norms,[39] more likely to engage in homosexual behavior, and less likely to marry someone of the opposite sex. Lastly, the *Adolescence* reports that children of homosexual parents are more likely to be molested than children in a heterosexual home.[40]

All of the information and statistics above point out that not only is the homosexual lifestyle not good for the individual, but same-sex "marriage" is a danger to the moral upbringing and common welfare of children.[41] As history has proven, traditional marriage is the best design for the family and fosters the greatest results among children. By adhering to the framework of traditional marriage, we can prevent that which would jeopardize our society and all of civilization. Therefore, a home that has both a father and mother provides children the best environment to develop spiritually, emotionally, physically, socially, and physiologically.[42]

Helping Homosexuals

As a student pastor for many years, I have been appalled at the lack of support churches offer people struggling with homosexuality. I remember one evening after preaching to a large group of young people, a young man was hanging around to talk with me. After I finished with the last student, he approached me cumbersomely with tears in his eyes. I asked him why he was crying, and he told me that he was in need of help. After asking some probing questions, this young man confessed that two teenage boys had molested him on two separate occasions. As I stood there stunned and trying desperately to console him, he proceeded to tell me that he was gay. Before I could say anything he abruptly pronounced that he knew homosexuality was wrong, had explained everything to his parents and was seeking help. Of course I reaffirmed the grace and forgiveness of Jesus Christ in his life, and gave him several programs that specialized in homosexual recovery for him and his parents. Unfortunately, that was the last I saw him.

It was that night after the young man left, that it hit me like a ton of bricks. Not only is the church relatively silent on this issue, but not many Bible believing churches have the proper resources that compare to the massively connected network homosexuals have for people like the young man I mentioned. The truth is there are very few churches that I could recommend in our local city that offered a Bible-based program designed to love and aid homosexuals through overcoming their addictive lifestyle. If parents want help for their child, they either need to pull out a loan to cover the entry fees into a professional clinic, or travel outside their comfort zone to find a program suitable for them.

As dangerous as homosexuality is, we are not to focus all of our attention on fallen creation but to look to the perfection of our Creator. I say this because the war isn't against homosexuals, as much as it is with those who commonly turn away from loving and obeying God. We need to be careful not to allow presumptuous behavior or verbal attacks to get the best of us when speaking about homosexuality, especially to homosexuals. This only stirs up more hostility and does nothing to solve the real problem of homosexuality.

Let me be clear. There is absolutely no place for mistreating or bullying of any kind towards homosexuals as individuals or as a community. I believe that defaming or humiliating someone who is gay is fueled by hatred and has no place in civil discourse. Instead, Christians need to confront the way homosexuals employ "victimization" as an attempt to wrangle public persuasion for their cause.

As Christians, we are to honor the fact that each human is made in the image of God, and therefore, is created equal. We need to remember that God has made each one of us diverse in color, in ethnicity, and in personality, and learn to appreciate the uniqueness and difference in each one of us. But that does not mean we are to apply this form of equality to the sexual predilections of homosexuals. Far too many Christians have taken this form of logic and applied it to homosexuality and same-sex "marriages." Homosexuality is a sexually immoral lifestyle that runs contrary to the Bible and is an abomination to God (Lev. 18:22; 20:13; Rom. 1:24-27; 1 Tm. 1:10; Jude 7). We are not to partake in its sinfulness nor are we to embrace the sinful choices of homosexuals. We are responsible for proclaiming the truth of God and modeling it to the world; a life that reflects the love, truth and grace of Jesus Christ (Eph. 5:1; Col. 4:5-6; 1 Pet. 3:15-16).

Christians need to be proactive in looking for ways to befriend homosexuals and evangelize them for Christ. We need to alert more of our churches to face the challenge of homosexuality head on and network with other agencies and organizations to educate and train families with the truth.[43] The more churches intentionally network across the nation, the more power and influence we will have in preventing homosexuals from the opportunity to indoctrinate our children in schools and hinder them from legalizing same-sex "marriage" in America.[44]

CHAPTER 10

Taking Back Our Family

~~~

"Our God will fight for us."
Nehemiah 4:20

T he war to destroy Christian families and values in America is certainly on the rise. Sadly, many Christians have abandoned their marriages for unbiblical reasons fueled by bitterness and self-indulgence. Though the church has experienced higher divorce rates and their influence in raising a godly family has significantly dropped in recent decades, we are not to give up and let the world tear our families asunder. Peter reminds us that God has called us out of the darkness into His wonderful light (1 Pet. 2:9-10), and urges to "abstain from sinful desires that wage war against your soul (2:11)."

You are called by God to fight and protect the sacredness of marriage and preserve the biblical building blocks that make up the family. But if you are going to take back your family for Christ in America, you definitely need to take a step back and make sure that your own marriage and family are reflecting the biblical standards given by God.

Biblical Marriage

One of the keys to living a strong biblical marriage is to know what it is. Married couples usually do not have a problem sharing their feelings and expressing a desire to meet each other's needs, but when it comes to understanding the model of marriage, silence fills the air. This may seem trivial, but I believe it explains a great deal as to why our marriages and families are so messed up. If people do not have any idea what the blueprint of marriage is, how then, do we expect them to live it?

The model of marriage is beautifully displayed in the New Testament. According to Paul, both the husband and the wife are to submit to one another in the fear of the Lord (Eph. 5:21). That is, they are to have mutual respect for one another and obediently exercise their differing roles and responsibilities with grace and harmony in a loving relationship before God. No individual person in the marriage is inherently inferior or superior to the other, but rather, equal in nature and uniquely designed by God (Gen. 1:27; Gal. 3:28). The wife is to show respect to her husband (Eph. 5:22; Col. 3:18), and the husband is to love and cherish his wife (Eph. 5:25; Col. 3:19). Marriages that lead their home with this kind of love and grace provide children a wonderful model of what it means to honor and obey (Pro. 1:8; Deut. 6:7; Eph. 6:1-3; Col. 3:20). Here's some practical insight that will help bring forth and sustain long lasting marriages in America.

First, the covenant between a husband and wife is a symbol of Christ and the church. Marriage is not about meeting your spouse half way, but it's about mutual submission under the authority and reverence of Christ (Eph. 5:21). Couples who get married because they believe their spouse "completes" them miss the biblical meaning of marriage. Marriage is not so much about the couples' likes and dislikes, but about loving and respecting one another based on the finished work of Jesus Christ. Paul writes, "complete my joy by being of the same mind, having the same love, being in full accord and of one mind. Do nothing from rivalry or conceit, but in humility count others more significant than yourselves. Let each of you look not only to his own interests, but also to the interests of others. Have this mind among yourselves, which is yours in Christ Jesus (Phil. 2:2-5)." What would marriages look like if their actions were lived out according to the mind of Christ?

Second, Christ gave up His life on the cross and died for our sins (Matt. 27:32-44; Rom. 3:24-26; 1 Pet. 3:18). This love is sacrificial and unconditional. It is the kind of love husbands are commanded to give to their wives (Eph. 5:25). Timothy Keller writes, "The reason that marriage is so painful and yet wonderful is because it is a reflection of the gospel, which is painful and wonderful at once."[1] Marriage will have its ups and downs, but by the grace of God couples are forgiven and can experience God's pleasures together.

And finally, marriage is about commitment. It is a commitment that recognizes the union between one man and one woman. Jesus stressed the permanence of marriage when He said, "What God has joined together let man not separate (Matt. 19:14)." It is a commitment to remain faithful and pure to your spouse alone (1 Cor. 6:15-17; Heb. 13:4) and remain committed to meeting their physical and spiritual needs as God intended (1 Cor. 13).

As you read in chapter six, many of the early American families exercised a fitting biblical model of marriage in their homes. Prior to our early settlers, the pathway to living a strong marriage goes back to ancient Jewish customs. Marriage, according to Jewish tradition, literally means "holiness and sanctification." When the husband and wife join themselves together as "one flesh" they are entering into a holy communion in the presence of God. Jewish teaching underscores how marriage symbolically unites a man and woman together in order to fulfill their destinies by complementing each other in the sight of God. Thus, the goal of marriage is to satisfy God by satisfying each other in devoted companionship. With a holy marriage devoted unto God, Jewish families seek to raise children as a blessing from God (Ps. 127). This is significant because in Jewish homes the ultimate goal is to live a holy and honorable life in the eyes of God (Lev. 11:44).

Traditional Jewish homes take seriously that parents are the primary teacher to impart religious truths and convictions for their children to respect and follow (Deut. 6; Ps. 78). The Ten Commandments places honoring the father and mother as a "bridge commandment" between obeying God and the responsibility to fellow man (Ex. 20:12). When children honor their parents, they are more likely to listen and learn to obey the law of God and live prosperous lives. In most traditional Jewish homes, every Friday night at the evening meal, the father blesses his sons, daughters, and reads Proverbs 31 in public honor of his wife.

How does your marriage stack up to the biblical model listed above? More than likely it needs some improvement, but the question is — will you do what it takes to live out this type of marriage? It is important to point out that the church needs to get its own marriages in order before it plans to have any real impact on the world. You can spend all your time correcting others and debating against divorce, cohabitation and same-sex "marriage," but it's all for naught unless you apply these biblical principles to your own life. The more marriages satisfy God rather than self, the more holiness and satisfaction will be gained in marriage. The more the husband loves his wife as Christ loved the church, the more enthusiastic she will be in honoring and respecting her husband (Eph. 5:33). Live out a strong marriage that is fulfilled in God so that your children can gain from it and experience the same.

Biblical Family

Through the years I have had the privilege of counseling with a variety of families. In these conversations, I have found that many families have lost sight of two simple truths: (1) who God is, and (2) His expectations for the family. Often, what I hear is how the other spouse never listens, or the arguments with the dreaded teenager, or how strict and controlling parents are at home. Whatever the case may be, one of the most fundamental principles every family must never forget is that God is holy (Ex. 15:11); and it's your duty to obey, honor and serve Him (Deut. 11:13). The moment you shift your focus back to God, the clearer and more effective you will be in ministering to the needs of your family.

The Bible teaches two key truths for fathers: (1) "do not provoke your children" (Eph. 6:4a); and (2) "bring them up in the training and admonition of the Lord" (Eph. 6:4b). Fathers need to always make it a top priority to be involved in their child's life. An involved father gives mom much comfort and lends wise counsel and security to children. Moreover, a father needs to be consistent. He needs to consistently avoid asserting his authority in a negative light. He needs to consistently teach, instruct, train, admonish, and discipline his family in the Word of God. That is, the father is to "nourish tenderly" his children and provide the proper tools and be the best example to develop them physically, mentally, spiritually, and socially. Ken Canfield (Founder of National Center of Fathering) said, "Fathering is not a sprint; it's a marathon." All of this takes time, so fathers don't give up!

Mothers are called to love and nurture their children (1 Thess. 2:7-8; Tit. 2:4). The love a mother has for her children is unparalleled. A nurturing mom provides the greatest love in the home. The love she has for her family is one of commitment, responsibility, caring, sensitivity, and wisdom. With all the duties and needs of the home, the selfless acts of moms are the greatest examples of Christ, and I believe, will produce the biggest rewards in heaven.

When the father and mother engage in their primary

responsibility to comfort, teach and discipline their children in the ways of God, children will grow up with a correct understanding of God, and live to honor Him. The sooner marriages turn back to God, the more effective they become to instill moral values in their families. The key is to build and sustain America on strong marriages that seek to raise children in the fear and admonition of the Lord.

re | shift Your Biblical Witness

I know this may seem overwhelming for most, but I pray Christians all over this great nation will begin to return to the right position, place and purpose that God intended for marriages, families and America. I can't stress enough how important a Christian's witness of marriage and family is to the world. I wholeheartedly believe that if more Christians were to return to exemplifying a godly marriage and raising their children the biblical way, our country would experience a great awakening. Before you plan to make a difference in the world, you need God's plan to make a difference in your own life.

As you seek to build a stronger marriage and loving family, always be aware of the evil forces that are strategically trying to destroy your foundation and witness in Christ.

May you and your family never abandon God or the essentials of His truth, nor forget the faith and values America was founded on and the importance to preserve them for future generations. Stop for a minute and pray that America will be filled with homes that have both parents actively rearing their children in loving marriages, and churches working to overturn abortion and provide a strong support system for those struggling with homosexuality. Undoubtedly, to shift back to the original purpose for America will require intense petitioning of God to reposition hearts and exchange old habits for new ones. The Bible says, "Do not throw away your confidence, which has great reward. For you have need of endurance, so that when you have done the will of God you may receive what is promised (Heb. 10:35-36)."

PART THREE

The War to Destroy
Our Country

CHAPTER 11

God-Given Rights

"It is for freedom that Christ has set us free."
Galatians 5:1

Thomas Jefferson penned the greatest and most profound words in all of American history when he opened the Declaration of Independence with this statement: "We hold these truths to be *self-evident*, that all men are *created equal*, that they are *endowed by their Creator* with certain *unalienable Rights*, that among these are *Life*, *Liberty* and the pursuit of *Happiness*. That to secure these rights, Governments are instituted among Men, deriving their just powers from the consent of the governed (emphasis added)." These unalienable rights are God-given and the main thrust for independent freedom from Great Britain and the declaration of American independence.

Natural Rights Ordained By God

John Locke's *Second Treatise* had a profound influence over the phrasing and organization of Jefferson's draft and finalization of the *Declaration of Independence*. Jefferson built upon the opening words of the Declaration of Independence from a belief that all individuals are held to a "Natural Law" or "Moral Law." Jefferson and the other drafters wanted to establish a political and governmental system aligned with the natural rights ordained by God and reflect the morality of individuals in the Declaration and, consequently, the U.S. Constitution. One particular source that had great significance to the drafters' belief in natural law as the guiding principle for American independence and governance came from William Blackstone's *Commentaries on the Laws of England*. In it, Blackstone revolutionized the landscape for Britain to construct a Constitution by arguing for self-government and the natural right to be free. He claimed, "This law of nature, being co-eval with mankind and dictated by God Himself, is of course superior in obligation to any other. It is binding over all the globe, in all the countries, and at all times: no human laws are of any validity, if contrary to this; and such of them as are valid derive all their force, and all their authority, mediately or immediately, from this original."[1]

In his widespread pamphlet, *The Farmer Refuted*, the young Alexander Hamilton argued in favor of the First Continental Congress by quoting from the infamous Blackstone and built upon this argument by stressing:

> Upon this law, depend the natural rights of mankind: the Supreme Being gave existence to man, together with the means of preserving and beatifying that existence. He endowed him with rational faculties, by the help of which, to discern and pursue such things, as were consistent with his duty and interest, and invested him with an inviolable right to personal liberty, and personal safety...The Sacred Rights of Mankind are not to be rummaged for, among old parchments, or musty records. They are written, as with a sun beam, in the whole volume of human nature, by the Hand of the Divinity itself; and can never be erased or obscured by mortal power.[2]

It is within the confines of this natural law that our Founders formulated both the Declaration of Independence and the U.S. Constitution, which was written to serve as the mechanism for protecting the God-given rights referenced in the Declaration. As such, one cannot understand and properly interpret the U.S. Constitution apart from understanding the Declaration, namely, that American independence and governance is based on the desire to protect God-given rights. In fact, as constitutional scholar Dr. Kevin Portteus explains, "Lincoln advocated a particular method of understanding the Constitution. He saw the document as the manifestation of a set of principles that guided the Founding Fathers in their understanding of law and nation making, and ought therefore to be employed by modern jurists in understanding the fruits of their labor. Lincoln believed and demonstrated that the Constitution must be interpreted in light of the principles of the Declaration of Independence to be interpreted correctly."[3]

Accordingly, accurate constitutional interpretation necessarily presupposes, and consequently implicates, a belief in God, in absolute (or self-evident) truth, and the right for every man and woman to freely engage in religious exercise. This was the instrumental guide of the Framers of the U.S. Constitution and the belief system constructed by the Founders of our great nation.

Our Founders built upon the dreams and beliefs of the early settlers and framed the U.S. Constitution around the God-given truths that all men are created equal and have the right to govern themselves as a sovereign people. It was within this governance that we have been given the right to life, liberty and the pursuit of happiness (including the liberties expressed in the Bill of Rights). Our Founders had strong conviction that equality of humanity retains and sustains the essence of human rights in a civil society. However, they also believed that if our natural rights were not exercised in accordance to the natural order, they would be abused beyond unnatural limitations.

The Drive to Live

According to the Bible, God is life and is the source of all life. David confessed, "My soul thirsts for God, for the living God (Ps. 42:2)." The prophet Jeremiah proclaimed, "But the Lord is the true God; He is the living God, the eternal King (Jer. 10:10)." As strong believers in God and the Bible, the Framers openly stated the right to life as the first of three self-evident truths bestowed by God our Creator. The unalienable right to life is one of the greatest qualities this nation was built on. It is pivotal to our very existence and a validation of God's love for His creation. Life is truly a great gift and blessing granted by God. And it is in this life that God directs us to live life freely and willingly in accordance with His moral standards.

The Founders' ideals were to construct a government that has the rightful power to protect the vitality of human life, but not the power to control or destroy it. Life (and its religious freedoms) are not a benevolent gift from the government, but inherent rights given to each person – whether an unborn child or a debilitated individual unable to care for himself. Each life is unique and specially designed by the sovereign plans of God to execute and fulfill divine purposes that bring honor and glory to Him. This is what the Bible teaches and is a powerful belief that our nation was founded upon.

The Drive to Be Free

Our Founders dared to dream big. They dreamed of establishing a free society of self-government, a society free from the scourge of tyranny. It was a dream that would motivate Thomas Jefferson to write the Declaration of Independence as a grievance to King George III. A dream that would ignite the American Revolution, fought and won by freedom-loving patriots. The Founders defended and believed in an ordered society that cherished and perpetuated freedoms of expression and religion. They did not believe that liberty required a diminution of religion in public life, but that every American had the natural right to worship God as they chose, and pursue a life with vast liberty and opportunity.[4] However, the Founders knew that without the continual protection of the free expression of freedom, it would not last. Thus, they erected the U.S. Constitution and branches of government to protect the rights of the people, but left it up to the people to maintain and sustain their freedoms. John Adams pointedly stated, "Posterity, you will never know how much it cost the present generation to preserve your freedom. I hope you will make good use of it. If you do not, I shall repent in heaven that ever I took half the pains to preserve it."[5]

The Drive to Achieve

In his classic work, *The Epic of America,* James Truslow Adams coined the phrase: "American Dream." Adams expressed his characterization of the American Dream with these sentiments,

> The American Dream is that dream of a land in which life should be better and richer and fuller for everyone, with opportunity for each according to ability or achievement. It is a difficult dream for the European upper classes to interpret adequately, and too many of us ourselves have grown weary and mistrustful of it. It is not a dream of motor cars

and high wages merely, but a dream of social order in which each man and each woman shall be able to attain to the fullest stature of which they are innately capable, and be recognized by others for what they are, regardless of the fortuitous circumstances of birth or position.[6]

This description of the "American Dream" came from the vision of what Thomas Jefferson and many of our Founders sought to achieve and preserve for all Americans. Many of our Founders believed in a country where a self-governing democracy could succeed in providing its citizens the liberties that would afford them opportunities to freely achieve a dream bigger than themselves. They believed in a country where the common man could be given the chance to make a better life for his family and be free to speak and share his faith without being persecuted.

Our Founders never intended for government to be the classifier of citizens according to rank and file. To our Founders, living the "American Dream" was to aspire for greatness and to pursue it wholeheartedly. The "American Dream" was not intended for the faint of heart nor built on the selfish ambitions of the individual, but on the drive that comes from honoring God and providing a safe place for family to live. As parents worked hard and cared for their families, they hoped and prayed that the future for their children would be bigger and brighter than their own.

CHAPTER 12

Threat #1: Remove the U.S. Constitution

"We, the people, are the rightful masters of both Congress and the courts; not to overthrow the Constitution, but to overthrow men who pervert the Constitution."[1] Abraham Lincoln

In the opening of the U.S. Constitution, it reads: "We the People of the United States, in Order to form a more perfect Union, establish Justice, insure domestic Tranquility, provide for the common defense, promote the general Welfare, and secure the Blessings of Liberty to ourselves and our Posterity, do ordain and establish the Constitution of the United States of America."

As we inspect the cultural landscape of America in the 21st century, it seems that our natural rights and the U.S. Constitution are being redefined to something other than what our Founders intended. This growing divide between traditionalism and cultural relativism has left many bruised and battered from substantial battles over truth and equal rights of individuals. As mentioned in chapter three, if cultural relativism becomes the dominant paradigm of the next generation in America, the U.S. Constitution will be null and void. In one corner stand the guiding principles of God's truth that set this nation on its course, stamping it with what goodness it may still possess. In the other is an unrestrained individual autonomy where human rights are redefined according to preference. This societal shift from the ideals America was founded upon has caused spiritual depravation and moral decay that breeds inequality and affects our freedoms. If the indispensible truths of the U.S. Constitution are removed, on what basis do we determine what standards are indicative to obey and what values and duties are imperative for Americans to follow?

Liberalism: The Constitution of Secularism

Liberalism is essentially an ideology that seeks to modify the U.S. Constitution and deconstruct the ideals of America and reform it with a utopian ideal centralized under the power of government. The liberals use several methods to bypass rational discourse and constitutionality in efforts to spread their propaganda. First, they attempt to overthrow all Judeo-Christian values and replace them with secularism. Second, they want to alter the U.S. Constitution to fit their secular and utopian analysis. Third, they restrict religious tolerance, except in the case of their own religious bias (i.e., secularism). Fourth, the liberal media likes to invoke their constitutional rights of free speech so they can twist the facts and spew their ideology freely and repeatedly.

According to Media Research Center (America's Media Watchdog), they reported a survey that was conducted in the mid-1990s under the title "The Media Elite Revisited." In a portion of their findings, they discovered that 97 percent of the media agreed that 'it is a woman's right to decide whether or not to have an abortion.' It also revealed that over 73 percent of the media elite approved of the homosexual lifestyle and felt it was comparable to heterosexual relationships. Finally, 75 percent of journalists who are actively reporting on the "news" everyday believe in in bigger government.[2]

The lack of objectivity in the media has become invaluable

to the liberal agenda. It is no longer about reporting what is actually news, but has become a platform for enforcing ideologies that skew the facts and for broadcasting lies. This infiltration of lies has had major ramifications in shaping people's false viewpoints of the role of government in American culture today. Because the mainstream media is currently at their disposal, along with hundreds of other liberal organizations and government agencies that push similar agendas, *society at large accepts what is false as authoritative and credible.*

However, as our First Amendment rights are being tested many Americans remain apathetic towards enacting change to help protect their God-given rights. This is due, in large part, to leaders that have bought into liberalism and have forfeited the priority to uphold the U.S. Constitution. Most of our elected officials have lost the fortitude to serve and represent the American people, and instead have put personal interests above the country. It is not unusual to find officials on every level more concerned with their own appearance or ambition than representing the community of people they were elected to serve and represent.

In *Legislating Morality*, Norman Geisler and Frank Turek write, "The Founders wrote into the Constitution checks and balances in an attempt to ensure that no governing body would wield too much power. Realizing that power corrupts, and absolute power tends to corrupt absolutely, the Founders intended for the people and the states to have most of the control."[3] This is exactly why the Framers felt so strongly about implementing a balance of powers that would lend accountability throughout the Executive, Legislative and Judicial branches of government, while establishing independent powers of each sovereign state. Our Founders believed the natural rights we possess are universal and absolute, and as such, no one person or institute has the moral authority to rule over or take away these rights away.

DECLARATION OF INDEPENDENCE	DECLARATION OF SECULARISM
Creator	*No* Creator
Created	Evolved
Self-evident truths	Self-*imposed beliefs*
Unalienable rights	*Transferable* rights

Proponents of liberalism know full well the checks and balances provided for and seek to undermine them. One particular area liberals have strategically targeted and successfully altered through the years is the Judicial Branch. This corruptive influence is manifest in the decisions of appointed judges whose legal interpretations draw from an extreme liberal worldview of relativism and naturalism. This constitutes a different interpretation from the Founder's intent and is a threat to the framework of the U.S. Constitution. As the courts continue to get stacked with more appointed liberal judges, this Branch will wield the power of imperial governance.

Unelected Judges: "We make the rules."

Theodore Roosevelt said, "It is the people, and not the judges, who are entitled to say what their constitution means, for the constitution is theirs; it belongs to them and not to their servants in office—any other theory is incompatible with the foundation principles of our government."[4] Do our judges today approach the U.S. Constitution with true objectivity? Do our federal judges, Ninth Circuit Court of Appeals, or even the U.S. Supreme Court abide under the fear of God anymore? My fellow Americans, it is no longer, "Of the *people* and by the *people*," but "Of the *judges* and by the *judges!*"

Judges do and ought to possess certain powers to govern

and rule on the cases presented before their courts. They are indeed conduits God has erected in society to uphold the law and enforce justice. However, with great power comes great responsibility. Just because judges are privileged to reside over the court of law, doesn't give them absolute power above the law. Judges are not rulers who can usurp the people's power and revoke their constitutional rights. Rather, judges ought to be models that stand for right and wrong before all people. A civil society needs to be able to trust that the judges over them realize their high courts are answerable to a higher Judge. Asaph declared, "And the heavens proclaim His [God's] righteousness, for God Himself is Judge (Ps. 50:6)."

In the best interest of our country, we need judges who rule beyond matters of personal preference, appeasement or pleasure. Unfortunately, many judges are liberal themselves as well as appointed by a liberal partisanship and retain loyalty to their backers. As a result, they rule favorably in furtherance of the liberal agenda. A prime example of this is Proposition 8 in California. This proposition (like so many throughout the country) was a state constitutional amendment of the California Marriage Protection Act. After the people of California voted to protect traditional marriage in their state, a liberal judge—who also happens to be a practicing homosexual—overturned the decision and reinstated gay marriage! Lou Sheldon, chairman and founder of the Traditional Values Coalition said in an interview with *Christianity Today*, that "It is an outrage that one arrogant and rogue federal judge can take it upon himself to overturn a centuries old definition of marriage and family ... Direct Democracy has been blatantly attacked today."[5]

But that's not all. A few more historic rulings demonstrate blatant abuse of judicial powers. In 1973, the U.S. Supreme Court overturned all laws against abortion in every state (Roe v. Wade); and in 2003 overturned all laws against sodomy in every state (Lawrence v. Texas). David Limbaugh gives an example of the hostility that most liberal judges exhibit toward Christianity. He wrote an article called, *The Judiciary's Culturally Sanctioned Allergy to Christianity Flourishes.* He tells of a case in Utah where the Tenth U.S. Circuit Court of Appeals banned a set of crosses near the side of public roads in honor of fallen state highway troopers as "unconstitutional." Limbaugh writes, "Our judiciary has become so obsessed with preventing any hint of a nod toward Christianity (it doesn't exhibit similar concerns about favoritism toward other religions or faith-based secular themes) that it has thwarted the driving purpose of the establishment clause."[6]

One may wonder how so many of our judges sitting on court benches across America have become so liberal. Let's examine the path they have traveled and see how liberalism has sullied most judges in the judicial system today. From a very early age the naturalistic education system taught them there is no God. Then they were taught that our Founders believed in a "make believe" deity that provided fictitious "unalienable rights." Along with this, prayer in schools was ruled unconstitutional, therefore, implying that God and religion is excluded from education. They learned to value religious diversity, to the exclusion of Christianity. Then the Ten Commandments and/or any religious symbol (i.e., cross) displayed in public was considered offensive to the nonreligious; and undermined the doctrine of separation of church and state. Finally, the Bible was considered a religious work of fiction filled with bigotry and bogus miracles. And that's only until they graduated high school.

The next phase of indoctrination continues in the universities. Professors are more liberal, anti-God, pro-abortion, and pro-gay & lesbian than ever before. Naturalism is the overarching worldview for virtually all subject matters at the university level. Students are analytically taught that morals are not up to a non-existent God or parents. Instead, the individual in the situation determines morals and relative truths. Life is all about what they want and feel it should be. By the time these students collect their college degree, the cement has hardened on the foundation of a new belief system that will drive their lifestyle, shape their values, and affect all future choices.

After receiving a degree from a secular university, matriculating students continue their education in law. In law school, "separation of church and state" becomes the creed for all future judges. Law students go through rigorous schooling for defending secular humanism. They are taught that any respectable judge should not tolerate talk of God, the Bible, or the Christian faith. Once law students graduate, they are branded as an elite liberal and issued power to rule on matters essential to the "living Constitution." Ingram makes note that, "Federal courts have usurped the rightful powers of Congress and state and local governments, labeling their preferred political solutions as newfound 'constitutional rights,' but then refused to protect us when governments launch illegal assaults on the true rights that are actually mentioned in the Constitution."[7] She goes on to write, "Many Americans don't realize the extent to which the Supreme Court has usurped power from the people and stolen the decision-making authority of elected officials on the state and federal level."[8]

In fear of the U.S. Supreme Court becoming an "imperial judiciary," Thomas Jefferson warned of the coming danger this could have on the newly liberated nation, "To consider the judges as the ultimate arbiters of all constitutional questions [is] a very dangerous doctrine indeed, and one which would place us under the despotism of an oligarchy."[9] Listed below are the two extreme contrasts of what Jefferson prophetically warned would happen if judges usurped too much power and acted over the U.S. Constitution.

CONSTITUTIONAL JUDICIARY	IMPERIAL JUDICIARY
Subordinate to Congress	*Above* Congress
Reaffirms the Constitution	*Reinterprets* the Constitution
Under the People	*Overrules* the People
Final Interpreter of the Law	*Final Arbiter* of the Law
Limited Power	*Unlimited* Power

Over time, the federal judges and the Supreme Court have gravitated noticeably toward imperial judiciary, far exceeding the boundaries our Founders intended for the Judicial Branch. Pat Robertson notes:

> If you think any of this happened by accident or that it's merely the natural evolution of the American justice system during the past two hundred years, think again. Ever since creating the right of judicial review in *Marbury v. Madison* in 1803, the Court has been absolutely giddy with its power. Justices addicted to the ideas of incremental change and social progress have been on a mission to transform the structures of American democracy. Along the way, the courts have invented rights and mandated social policies that are completely outside the bounds of the Supreme Court's legitimate function or authority. They have alienated millions; given aid to criminals, sociopaths, and social engineers; and erected obstacles to law and order that trouble every city and state, and cloud the future of the Republic.[10]

With this social engineering by judges acting as ultimate arbiters on all matters of life, it is easy to see how absolute corruption eventually corrupts absolutely. Listed below are cases ranging back as far as 1948 that demonstrate the trend liberal judges have taken to remove God and Christianity:

McCollum v. Board of Education **(1948)**	Banned Religious Instruction on School Property
Engel v. Vitale **(1962)**	Banned Prayer in Schools
Abington Sch. Dist. v. Schempp **(1963)**	Banned Bible Reading in Schools
Stone v. Graham (1980)	Banned The Ten Commandments in Schools
United States v. Eichman **(1990)**	Overturned Flag Protection Act
Santa Fe Indep. Sch. Dist. v. Doe **(2000)**	Banned Prayer at Sporting Events
Ashcroft v. Free Speech Coalition **(2002)**	Overturned Child Pornography Protection Act

In the end, America is faced with a major threat when it comes to constitutional rights. Judges are no longer holding to an honorable post or residing over the bench with the sole purpose to enact justice and protect the common interests of Americans. Instead, we have judges who are dishonoring their posts by overriding the three branches. This is criminal, not judicial! As the brilliant Edmund Burke once said, "Bad laws are the worst sort of tyranny."[11] And America has had more than its fair share of bad laws.

This is why a defense of the U.S. Constitution is of utmost importance. Mark Levine writes, "If the Constitution's meaning can be erased or rewritten, and the Framer's intentions ignored, it ceases to be a constitution but is instead a concoction of political expedients that serve the contemporary policy agendas of the few who are entrusted with public authority to preserve it."[12] To Levine's point, if liberal judges are successful in removing the U.S. Constitution, then our founding principles are nothing more than antiquated jargon, not self-evident truths bestowed by God.[13] This being the case, the U.S. Constitution will continue to be defragmented and altered into a secularized text without recognition of natural law or mention of a Divine Creator.

The U.S. Constitution is indispensable to American society. It contains truths that undergird the moral foundation that directs our conduct and guides our moral and public lives, for individuals and government alike. If tampered with and replaced, America will see corrupt power at its worst. We need to obstruct this injustice for the sake of our children's futures.

Holding Judges Accountable

If we are going to limit the abuse of judicial powers, we must take action against their public attacks against God and their removal of Him in the court of law. Our rights come from God, not judges. What course of action can we take? We must hold our judges accountable to the foundational truth of the U.S. Constitution. We need judges to be guided by the law, not presiding over the law. I have stressed this point for years while teaching: If there is no God, then who makes the ultimate call in determining what is right or wrong?

As Jefferson once wrote in defense of a higher standard, "...their rights as derived from the laws of nature, and not as the gift of their Chief Magistrate."[14] Our judges have come to believe that they are the supreme lawmakers in our country and this is a serious problem today. God is the Ultimate Judge, not man. With this kind of control and power, liberal judges routinely assault the constitutional rights of Americans by citing international law as though it trumps the Moral Law.

We must train up more young Christians to fill prominent positions that will influence our country for the better. We need veto power within both houses of Congress to retain checks and balances so that the U.S. Supreme Court cannot freely undermine the U.S. Constitution. We need to take action to prevent judges overruling the sanctity of marriage and life. We need to assemble watchdogs in communities across the country and crack down on judges who usurp the U.S. Constitution. No more tenure for secular radicals who are releasing child molesters, convicted criminals, overturning propositions, and telling the American people what they deem "unconstitutional." What is unconstitutional is unelected judges ruling on cases based on bias opinions, and not according to the letter of the law.

CHAPTER 13

Threat #2: Redefine Government

"The Constitution is not an instrument for the government to restrain the people, it is an instrument for the people to restrain the government – lest it come to dominate our lives and interests."[1] Patrick Henry

Unfortunately, the "American Dream" has lost its original focus and undergone a makeover. The "American Dream" was once believed to bring a better life to those who pursued it, but now it has warped into the American nightmare where Americans fear they are pursuing a dead end. Perhaps this is because the Dream was once believed to be bigger and better than the one pursuing it, and now the Dream is centered on the person who believes they are bigger and better than life itself.

No longer is it about the Christian heritage of the country, the lives and faith of the people, nor the expressions of community and harmony. And because of this, the ever-expanding and self-indulgent way of life for most Americans has been put on the endangered list. With the political persuasion and control from the unions and welfare programs, many American people have become enslaved to their own lustful desires. Never realizing that the more they feed their passions and desires, the further indebted they become to the high price tags and heavy interest they carry.

What most Americans fail to realize is that individualism has lasting effects on nationalism. That is, what we do *individually* impacts what happens *nationally*. The state of our home sheds light on the state of affairs in our country. The predictive book *The Great Gatsby* is an excellent piece that tells the story of what pride, individualism, and self-pity can do to a person. The naivety of Jay Gatsby's self-individualistic dream to become rich and highly successful blinded him from actually achieving a life worth living. He believed that wealth and power was the measure of success and happiness, and yet, as the story goes, dies a miserable man in the end. One can easily translate the fatality of Gatsby to that of our declining country.

Socialism: The 'Collective Salvation' Movement

Essentially, there are two opposing and competing economic strategies that attempt to influence the financial market: socialism and capitalism. Socialism, simply put, is fueled by Marxism and embraces communism as the ideal economic system. It gives government the power to control production and distribute resources, which would (in theory), be owned in common by a classless society. Alternatively, capitalism is a belief in a free market exchange, whereby the people have private ownership and have the right to buy, sell, and trade in hopes to make a profit; a market-system championed and fought for by our Founders.

There are two essential disagreements socialism has with capitalism. Karl Marx (1818-1883), the great revolutionary communist, explained capitalism as the, "Accumulation of wealth at one pole is, therefore, at the same time accumulation of misery, agony of toil, slavery, ignorance, brutality, mental degradation, at the opposite pole."[2] According to Marx, the system of capitalism exploits workers because products are sold at prices higher than the cost to manufacture. A socialist would say that the worker is being ripped off or devalued because the private owner is selling his product for more than it is worth and not giving the workers equal or more pay based on the profit margin. In essence, the capitalist is using and manipulating workers by hiring them as cheap labor while reaping all the benefits.

The second problem socialism has with a capitalistic system is that it creates too much confusion and chaos within the industry. Socialism argues from the premise that if you have buyers and sellers all simultaneously manufacturing and selling their goods, while at the same time servicing their product at different levels of value, you have chaos. Karl Marx attempted to demonstrate that capitalism (if left to its own devices) would continue to inhibit the world's ability to achieve the overall economic climate of success, and would eventually destroy itself.Vladimir Lenin (1870-1924) shared these views of Marx and sought to establish a Proletariat Revolution in Russia. He accomplished this by becoming the dictatorial ruler of the Union of Soviet Socialist Republic. His socialistic outlook viewed capitalism as poor economics because it supported private property and free market exchange. Lenin's idea was to implement an equal playing field for workers who are working together for a common purpose, not in competition of one another. Combined, this Marxist-Leninist philosophy held that to have real success you must have a planned economy to discover the best methods of production and distribution. Their plan was to allow capitalism to ultimately lead to its foreseen downfall, and afterward, usher in their method of a new socialistic system. Their goal for the future of the world was to institute a utopia in which the ownership of all resources for production (property and businesses) would be commonly owned by a classless society.

The evil dictator who embodied the naturalistic philosophy and socialistic ideology of Marx and Lenin was Joseph

Stalin (1878-1953). He became the supreme ruler of the Soviet Union after the death of Lenin in 1924. Stalin's ideal world consisted of workers given the certainty of work with equal pay. This idea became known as the Communist Utopia. It is a belief that the bigger the government, the more redistribution of wealth, benefits and freedoms people will be able to experience. Thus, in this communist society, the working conditions, housing, property, production and distribution, agriculture, laws, and a nationally planned economy would all be under the control of the government.

BIG GOV'T: "We own you."

When we examine current and historical scenarios where cultural relativism, liberalism, and socialism prevail with respect to government, we find their aggregate yield is always "BIG GOV'T." In the past, most Americans had a basic understanding that BIG GOV'T didn't equal better government. In their view, BIG GOV'T had inherent problems that had a tendency to over-burden, over-tax and over-reach its authority with regard to the rights of the people. But that perception of BIG GOV'T has but come and gone.

In the last century, liberalism has become a big player in nullifying the checks and balances of our government with its heavy-handed influence in Washington and dominating most legislative and judiciary processes throughout government today. In the end, this relativistic mindset (and its policies) would supposedly build a "brighter future for America" via BIG GOV'T — more bureaucracy, more control, more power, more authority in the hands of the federal government.

However, what is being overlooked is that America was never built on the concept of BIG GOV'T. Why? Because our Founders knew that BIG GOV'T begets tyranny. With BIG GOV'T come less *governance* of the people and more *governing* by a bureaucratic system. Ultimately we relinquish control of our constitutional rights to BIG GOV'T and make it the arbitrator of nearly every aspect of our lives! It's tragic to think that America, once a deliverer of nations from tyranny, is now battling despotism on its own soil.[3]

The following chart outlines key differences between limited government and BIG GOV'T:

LIMITED GOVERNMENT	BIG GOV'T
The Constitution of the United States	The Communist Manifesto
George Washington; James Madison; Thomas Jefferson; John Adams	Karl Marx; Friedrich Engels; Joseph Stalin; Vladimir Lenin
Capitalism	Socialism
Power to the People	Power to One Man
Prosperity, Freedom & Progress	Poverty, Death & Destruction

So the government that began as merely a watchdog has now become a Leviathan. BIG GOV'T is an enormous beast that consumes everything in its path. How will the United States remain a Republic if BIG GOV'T gets so big that it becomes the supreme arbitrator, creditor, collector, lender, employer, insurer, consumer, and spender? The more we allow BIG GOV'T to get bigger, the more out of control it becomes and the more control it has over our lives. Right now we are being overpowered by BIG GOV'T and are presently losing more of our liberties each day. Since God has preordained us as citizens in this country at this time, we must do everything within our power to protect our freedoms and slay the Leviathan of BIG GOV'T in America.

To put the oversized and overzealous into proper

context, let's examine the average life of an American and see how much regulation comes from BIG GOV'T. For starters, BIG GOV'T regulates every permit necessary prior to building a home, every piece of material used to build a home, and every item placed in the home upon completion. But the regulation doesn't end there. BIG GOV'T regulates food, medical supplies, vitamins, hygiene products, clothing, cleaning supplies, and entertainment devices. All our vehicles, recreational toys, restaurants, schools, and doctors' offices have all been forced to comply with certain regulations of BIG GOV'T. If BIG GOV'T regulates everything we own and do, are we really free? This should be a huge concern to all Americans because it doesn't end there.

There are many issues that BIG GOV'T would like to pile onto the bureaucracy, but we will specifically look at three fundamentally bad regulations of BIG GOV'T and the devastating effects they have on our economy, healthcare and environment.

BIG GOV'T Debt: "Print more money."

The legendary economist and professor, John Taylor writes, "At its most basic level, economic freedom means that families, individuals, and entrepreneurs are free to decide what to produce, what to consume, what to buy and sell, and how to help others."[4] He goes on to explain five keys to restoring America's prosperity. I have given a summary of each key point.

1. *Predictable policy framework* — Follow the trend of individual economic freedom.
2. *Rule of law* — Stick to free market principles and drive up the entrepreneurial spirit and innovation to create jobs.
3. *Strong incentives* — Don't rely on government

intervention but on incentives that inspire growth.

4. *Reliance on markets* — Stay away from manipulating the market and stimulus spending.
5. *Clearly limited role for government* — Reduce federal control and wasteful spending.[5]

Common sense tells us that spending more money than available, combined with high interest rates, will rapidly lead to massive debt accumulation, and eventually bankruptcy. The current debt of our nation is based on policy makers abandoning these five keys of economic stability, and consequently, poses a formidable threat to our national security.

Remember the difference between capitalism and socialism? Capitalism is built on a free-market system, competiveness, entrepreneurship, and gains and losses. Socialism, on the other hand, is a carefully controlled system that divests the rights of individuals to increase in wealth or gain for the sake of equality of the community as a whole. This is exactly what BIG GOV'T is. It seeks to control the economy through regulations, wage and price controls, stimulus packages, quantitative easing, and higher taxes. Instead of getting a boost, followed by long-term economic growth, the interference of BIG GOV'T has only debilitated the free market and destroyed the entrepreneurial spirit of small businesses.

Reality check: *Is it really worth giving into more greed when all we have to show for it is more debt?* It is dismal to watch our great nation, which has been so fortunate and blessed by God, become the most bankrupt nation on the planet. Not only can we not afford most of the life we live in America, but more importantly, our children can't afford to inherit the pile of debt accumulated by wasteful spending by our nation's leaders. Our addiction and greed, fueled by the pursuit for more happiness, has devalued our relationships with our families, and caused more anxiety, loneliness and regret.

BIG GOV'T Healthcare: "Doctors' Orders."

Does the U.S. Constitution say that all Americans need to be insured? Does the U.S. Constitution force Americans to purchase universal health care? No, it doesn't! Yet, liberals have managed, once again, to strip us of our protected rights under the U.S. Constitution and mandate that states issue health care coverage even though the overwhelming majority of Americans continuously vote against universal health care! A quick review of the failed nationalized healthcare in Britain and Canada ought to have been proof enough for American politicians to vote otherwise. In addition, how does the government plan to keep consumer costs down while providing exceptional health care when Social Security, Medicaid, and Medicare are all bankrupt?

What does this mean for the future of our children? BIG GOV'T is demolishing our free-market health care system and replacing it with a bureaucratic one. Our children will no longer have a right to choose their own personal health care coverage or their physician. If they choose not to purchase universal healthcare, they will receive penalties and fines, and accrue even more mounting debt.

Accordingly, there will be fewer doctors because of the spending cuts. This translates into longer wait times and higher premium costs for specialists. Socialized health care means our children get more BIG GOV'T, which translates into fewer freedoms for them and more debt to pay off. It means the fate of the elderly, the mentally challenged, or those waiting for transplants will be the last to receive care, which translates to more loss and devaluing of life. BIG GOV'T is not interested in the *health* of Americans, but only interested in controlling the *wealth* of Americans.

BIG GOV'T Energy Plan: "Save the planet."

America has seen a great shift in the past century on the issue of the environment. An agency entrusted to protect the environment now has the power to limit where we can go, what we can eat, and what we can buy. Who would have thought that America would be so shackled as a result of the Environment Protection Agency (EPA)? We are told that humans are overpopulating the earth and a cancer to the planet. The EPA (with the help of many radical environmentalists and activists) inundates the media with doomsday reports predicting the coming of a great ecological apocalypse. Then BIG GOV'T feels obligated to step in and do whatever necessary to prevent this from happening to planet earth.

America has bought into the lie that planet earth (environment) is a thing to be worshipped; putting the needs of Mother Earth above the recognized needs of humans to survive. We see this pattern recorded in the Bible. Paul writes to the Romans, "They exchanged the truth about God for a lie, and worshiped and served created things rather than the Creator—who is forever praised. Amen (Rom. 1:25)." The Bible is clear that God is the Creator of the universe and has given us charge to be good stewards of the environment. From the beginning God placed Adam over creation to rule over it. And as such, he and his descendants became God's representative on the earth (Gen. 1:28; 9:1, 7).

But the EPA does not share this viewpoint. BIG GOV'T is the ruling class and has the power, right and duty to restrict and regulate any person, business, or entity from endangering Mother Earth. This certainly has become a dangerous proposition in America. The more a regulatory system (like the EPA) mixes up the created order the less likely it will abide by the rules of God. This being the case, the EPA will eventually add to the demise of America rather than helping it. They believe more bureaucracy and tighter restrictions will lead to a more prosperous and bio-friendly environment. Yet what they don't realize is that some of the most polluted and toxic places in the world are in communist countries like China and Russia. Their communistic regulations and complete bureaucratic takeover has created more pollution and toxic waste than clean energy.[6]

The EPA continues to gobble up more real estate and deny even more businesses the ability to create jobs. Rather than explore, drill and produce our own oil and gas with American resources, the EPA continues to restrict the exploration of new natural resources with moratoriums. This forces America to rely more heavily on foreign oil and send enormous amounts of money to Arab nations, with no end in sight. This affects our economic stability as well as our national security. In regards to our economy, the EPA applies unachievable emission restrictions on coal plants, curtails domestic oil exploration and production, and erects permit processes too costly and complicated for companies to attain. This directly impacts national security by driving up the national debt, stifling job growth, reducing the defense budget for more eco-friendly programs, remaining dependent on foreign oil, and constricting the rights and liberties of private citizens.[7]

The Natural Resources Defense Council reports, "America's oil habit not only pinches our pockets and fuels OPEC's rising profits, but it also threatens our economy, national security and environment. According to the Department of Energy, the United States currently uses nearly 20 million barrels of oil a day, importing 55 percent of it. We spend more than $20 billion each year on oil from the Middle East. Twenty years from now, U.S. consumption will rise to 28.3 million barrels of oil a day, with 70 percent imported. This heavy reliance on foreign oil makes America increasingly dependent on some of the least stable, undemocratic countries in the world."[8]

With our dependency on foreign oil and unsettling news

daily from the Middle East, America is jeopardizing its future safety. And as more hostility arises and the regional instabilities escalate, the demand for oil will rise and push the price to all-time highs. Subsequently, the more BIG GOV'T forbids the U.S. from producing and supplying our own natural resources, the more inclined we are to bend at the mercies of Arab nations, and risk annihilation in the not so distant future. Iran is becoming a very strong force in the Persian Gulf and a larger owner and supplier of the world's oil market. They currently possess the second-largest reserve of oil in the world, which is larger than those of Iraq and second only to Saudi Arabia.[9] Additionally, Russia is supplying Iran with weapons and nuclear technology, and is in the process of assisting them in building over twenty nuclear plants. At this pace, Iran will become the first Arab nation to possess nuclear weapons. Just think what effect this will have if Iran achieves nuclear supremacy in the Middle East.[10]

Returning to Proper Government

As mentioned previously, if more Americans become hooked on the despotic consumption of BIG GOV'T, it will soon enough become the sole enterprise that delivers welfare to all Americans. The chart below provides a brief summary of the two ideologies.

BIBLICAL IDEOLOGY	SOCIALISTIC IDEOLOGY
Hard Work	Entitlements
Productivity	Unions and Bureaucracy
Elected Representation	Bureaucrats and Judges
Honesty	Corruption
Limited Government with Low Taxes	BIG GOV'T with High Taxes

Privately Controlled Property	Government Controlled Property
Religious Freedom	Secular Oppression

Throughout history, the free enterprise of capitalism has proven to be the most beneficial and profitable organism for any society or country around the world. Capitalism is the only economic system where freedom and prosperity can be achieved. The Bible clearly demonstrates that economic competition brings advantages and prosperity in a capitalistic society. First, the Bible grants that people ought to be given free access to own private land and be good stewards of their resources (Acts 5:1-4). Second, a free enterprise system bears the opportunity for success and fortune (Eph. 4:28). Third, a free market exchange thrives on competition and individuality (Pro. 14:23; Lk. 10:7).[11]

Furthermore, socialism is built on the distrust of the free market strategy and relies on a planned economy that is run by an increase of political power and governmental oversight. Not only does it have power to control the pricing, production, and distribution of goods and services, but socialism also dictates the daily lives of the people. This creates severe problems for the success of socialism. In a pure capitalistic system, it is the people who freely determine the prices and procedures in selling their products in a free market. Marxism stressed that capitalism was nothing more than a wealthy few that hoarded all the money and left nothing for the rest, which is simply false. It is under capitalism that the rich contribute towards the needs of the poor through their wealth and investments that produce other wealth, which creates jobs. When comparing the two economic strategies side-by-side, we realize that it is the economic strain of socialism under which people are predominantly oppressed and will most likely lead to poverty.

In 1918, Marxists rapidly ushered socialism into Russia,

successfully seizing all private land from the people. The result was devastating. By 1921 the situation was dire and the national economy was in shambles. Lenin began to threaten and imprison his own people, even to the point of killing millions. Once Russia was in complete ruins (due to Lenin's socialized plan), Lenin reverted back to the principles of capitalism to restore the infrastructure of his country. Hence, the result of socialism was a failed attempt to deliver its promise of a Communist Utopia, which ultimately led to the demise of a nation.

Marxism fails to pinpoint a time in history where socialism has demonstrated a classless society. What they got instead was a dictatorship that stripped them of their rights, murdered millions of people, and destroyed all hope of achieving financial success. History has proven that a utopian society is an impossible dream that will never bring positive change to the world; in fact quite the opposite. The classless society is also a contradiction because socialism breeds two classes of individuals: the poor class and the dictatorship class. In his book, *Prosperity and Poverty*, Calvin Beisner proves this point, "The only way to arrive at equal fruits is to equalize behavior, and that requires robbing men of liberty, making them slaves."[12]

Capitalism, on the other hand, has convincingly proven its worth and success. You can see how powerful and vibrant the United States and Europe has been throughout history due in large part to capitalism as their form of government and economics. There is no doubt that a free market exchange that supports the idea of private property and free enterprise is the most successful strategy for any form of government to achieve financial success and provide the opportunity of all people to govern their own lives.

Opportunity vs. Outcome

The great American economist and recipient of the Nobel Prize of Economics, Milton Friedman once said, "A society that puts equality before freedom will get neither. A society that puts freedom before equality will get a high degree of both."[13] The former is true of socialism.

Although the fight for equal outcomes may appear just, the strategy to achieve this seriously flawed goal is damaging the country. One of the problems is that equality of outcome necessitates a guaranteed level of outcome. Foisting equality of outcome over opportunity actually strips people of equal rights, creating policies and regulations that serve to restrict freedoms of Americans. This is thinly veiled socialism and is part of the liberal agenda.

Contrary to the Founders, socialism champions redistribution of wealth, anti-discrimination laws, and equal "opportunity" programs that level the playing field for the "have-nots." The idea that all Americans must be given equal allowance and rank is quickly turning our country into an egalitarian society. This has become a forceful maneuver to try and convince the current generation to exchange their individual liberty and property for an egalitarian ideal that says all people must receive equal pay, education, talent, and so forth. However, there are several problems with the concept of equality of outcome.

First, nowhere in the U.S. Constitution, Bill of Rights or the Federalist Papers is there any mention of equality of outcome. The reason for that is simple: our Founders did not believe in it. They believed in the dignity, equality, and inherent rights of individuals as a gift of God, but that is not to mean everyone has equal talents and outcomes. The brilliant legal mind of John Adams addressed the subject of equality in his *Discourses on Davila*. In it he says, "Although, among men, all are subject by nature to equal laws of morality, and in society have a right to equal laws for their government, yet no two men are perfectly equal in person, property, understanding, activity, and virtue, or ever can be made so by any power less than that which created them."[14]

Furthermore, equality of outcome leads to more class *welfare* because of the constant barrage of class *warfare* that aims to get more entitlements and government handouts. As a result, Congress has misallocated resources to people based on race, color and alternative lifestyle, and not on experience, education, and aptitude. Robison and Richards stress, "When government tries to substitute itself for the proper functions of business, enterprise, and the market, it does more harm than good, distorts natural incentives, encourages cycles of dependency, replaces the happiness of earned success with the subtle indignity of a handout, hinders the creativity of entrepreneurs, and turns the win-win game of a free exchange into a win-lose game of coercion and redistribution."[15] It is not the government's responsibility to reserve spots for the less fortunate; but rather, it is up to the individual to be responsible, work hard, and hopefully earn the right to be happy in their success.

Lastly, do we apply equality of outcome when it comes to sports? Not a chance. As fans, we demand the best. We want to know that the players wearing that uniform or the musician singing that hit song are the best money can buy. We don't waste our time with mediocrity in the professional arena. We want to know that professional athletes and performers worked hard to earn that spot. And, guess what? That's the American way! If someone believes he has what it takes to be the next Steve Jobs, then all he needs to do is devote his time, energy, money, passion, creativity, and innovation to be the next great success. Consequently, equality of outcome destroys the opportunity for people to succeed in their own dreams, talents and ambitions.

CHAPTER 14

Threat #3: Replace Freedoms

"The liberties of our country, the freedom of our civil constitution, are worth defending at all hazards; and it is our duty to defend them against all attacks."[1] Samuel Adams

As the U.S. Constitution continues to be reduced to mere words subject to liberal interpretation and our government becoming less of a Republic, it will only be a matter of time before the freedoms we partake will be replaced with little or no freedoms at all. A grave consequence to this constant war is the ever-growing concern and present threat of illegal immigration.

Illegal Immigration: "Forget laws."

America is a nation of immigrants. In years past, most immigrants came to this country and followed the immigration laws and became law-abiding citizens of the United States of America. However, today, our nation's political powers are unilaterally reforming the immigration laws, and sanctioning millions of "illegal aliens" (official legal term in the U.S. codes and provisions) the "right" to reside in America. As a hotly debated and sensitive matter to most, I want to be clear from the start that I do not condone or condemn immigrants the right or opportunity to come to the United States of America. As a descendant of immigrants from Mexico, and a born and bred Arizonian, the issue of immigration is one dear to my heart.

I have had my fair share of hotly contested debates about illegal immigration among Christians and others alike. Unfortunately, far too many Christians (including pastors) are incapable of articulating a rational discussion on the laws and policies of immigration (both legally and illegally), let alone offer a biblically sound point of view. This is certainly an important topic to rigorously discuss and get our hands dirty (if needed) because lives are at stake. This is why we need to discuss the issue objectively and reasonably and not allow our subjectivity to get in the way of the plain facts. However difficult and emotional illegal immigration may be we can't afford to allow it to run amuck. There is an underlining threat posed by illegal immigration that if left unresolved, will in fact destroy our country as we know it.

Abusing Our Laws and Freedoms

The truth is illegal immigration is rapidly worsening in our country and within the past several decades has brought far more problems than solutions. This is a serious matter that directly affects the safety of our homeland, and thus one we cannot overlook. The fact remains no nation can and will survive if their borders are left wide open and their laws are not being enforced.[2] Patrick Buchanan put it plainly, "America is being invaded, and if this is not stopped, it will mean the end of the United States."[3]

Mike Huckabee gives clarifying reasoning on the dangerous threat posed by illegal aliens:

> Most of today's illegal immigrants bear little resemblance to their predecessors from previous generations. We can no more fault a man or woman for wanting to live

in the United States than we can fault our own forefathers who sought a better future here. However, when our forefathers came to America, it was to be Americans — to live here and become a part of the fabric of this great country. In too many cases, illegal border crossers have no intention or desire to spend their lives in America but are coming simply for economic gain, to make money to send back to their families in Mexico or Central America. This creates a shadow culture living "off the grid," never truly putting down roots in this country.[4]

As described by Huckabee, this is the heart of the discussion. We need to examine and realize the real dangers if left ignored. The issues related to illegal aliens consist of (but are not limited to) taking our liberties for granted, looking for government bailouts, getting free medical care, finding cheap labor, attaining free education, and receiving free housing allowances. In essence, we have created a frivolous system whereby millions upon millions of illegals are able to unreservedly cross our unsecure borders with no intent to become American citizens and no desire to be patriots of the freedoms our countrymen fought and gave their lives for. Many illegal aliens cross our borders, leaving millions of tons of trash and waste; enter our country illegally and then disrespect our laws and way of living. We are witnessing a hijacking of the freedoms and constitutional rights of Americans for an all-expense paid trip on the taxpayer's dime. The longer we wait to reinforce our immigration laws, devise a plan to help improve the immigration process (locally and federally), and beef up the security of our borders, the sooner we will be overrun by the power and size of millions of illegals.

In March of 2007, the U.S. Census Bureau showed that our nation's immigrant population (legal and illegal) rose to 38 million. They estimate that over 12 million of these immigrants are of illegal status.[5] To have millions of illegals flying under the radar with no profile or known history is alarming, and is a direct threat to national security, our families, and way of life.

Crimes Committed By Illegal Aliens

As the illegal population in America increases, so has the crime. The crime committed by illegal aliens has become a major problem for federal and local authorities as well as federal, state and local prisons. District Attorney John M. Morganelli appeared before the House Subcommittee on Immigration, Border, Security and Claims and brought forth this troubling testimony:

> Unfortunately, the majority of illegal aliens who are here are engaged in criminal activity. Identity theft, use of fraudulent social security numbers and green cards, tax evasion, driving without licenses represent some of the crimes that are engaged in by the majority of illegal aliens on a daily basis merely to maintain and hide their illegal status. In addition, violent crime and drug distribution and possession is also prevalent among illegal aliens. Over 25% of today's federal prison population is illegal aliens. In some areas of the country, 12% of felonies, 25% of burglaries and 34% of thefts are committed by illegal aliens.[6]

Here are a few additional criminal statistics caused by the rising population of illegal aliens in the United States:

- In 2007, the Pew Hispanic Center discovered that Latinos accounted for 40% of all sentenced federal offenders, more than triple their share of the total U.S population. This is an increase of over 24% since early 1991 (according to the United States Sentencing Commission).[7]
- In 2011, the Border Patrol apprehended 447,500 illegal immigrants along the southwest border.
- An estimated 12 Americans are murdered everyday by illegal aliens; which translates to 4,380 every year. Illegal aliens driving drunk kill an additional 13 Americans every day; which translates to 4,745.[8]
- An average of 93 sex offenders and 12 serial sexual offenders come across U.S. borders every day. This conservative estimation arrives at the figure of 240,000 offenders entering the U.S every year.[9]
- It is estimated that there is 1.4 million gang members in the U.S, and almost half are made up of Hispanic descent. Approximately 90% of U.S. MS-13 (violent Salvadoran gang) members are foreign-born illegal aliens.[10]
- The Justice Department estimates that the Mexican and Colombian cartels operate in over 1,286 U.S. cities and take in an average of $18 billion to $39 billion dollars from the U.S. every year.[11]

These disturbing facts have also brought considerable concern to our major security departments of the United States. According to a Majority Staff Report of the House Committee on Homeland Security, it found that not all illegal aliens are coming to the United States to find work. Many law enforcement agencies indicate that large numbers of illegals are dangerous criminals fleeing their home countries to take refuge in the United States. That means wanted criminals are entering the United States under the radar with no known identities or whereabouts.[12]

Costs Amassed By Illegal Aliens

Rather than go through immigration and pay their dues, illegals send billions of dollars back to their homeland and cost taxpayers billions of dollars to fund their stay. The Federation for American Immigration Reform (FAIR), a leading research organization in the field of immigration, estimated that illegal labor costs Americans anywhere from $30 to $50 billion every year. That's $3 to 4 billion a month! FAIR also found that illegal immigration costs the states over $80 billion and the federal government over $20 billion to cover the growing expenses of medical care, work wages, education, and the prosecuting and incarcerating of illegal aliens. Approximately 48 percent of illegal aliens in America are uninsured and federal laws require all hospitals to provide care and treatment.[13] This means that state and local taxpayers foot the bill every time an uninsured illegal alien goes to the hospital.

The cost associated with illegal immigration is a massive burden our nation cannot afford to bear much longer. Yet while this nearly insurmountable drain increases daily, American borders lack proper funding and security and coastlines are not patrolled thoroughly. Despite these well-documented issues, many elected officials show incredible leniency or a lackadaisical attitude toward illegal immigration, taking little or no action to rectify its threat.

Gaps in Our Borders and System

It's not only border security that needs to be addressed, but also our inadequate system of monitoring and tracking illegal immigrants. Terrorist groups such as Al-Qaeda are looking for ways to cross the Mexican border into the United States. If we consider the major holes within our own immigration service and security regarding the 9/11 hijackers, we discover they all had expired visas! Our failed visa system is a direct link to how these illegals remain indefinitely in America without a second glance.

At the same time, what does it merit to tighten our borders if we continue to tolerate politicians who push for amnesty, courts throwing out illegal alien cases, companies breaking illegal labor laws, state colleges funding illegal immigrants, and banks opening accounts for illegal aliens? With the lack of enforcement of immigration laws and underfunded border protection, there is no end in sight to the millions of illegals flooding our borders, overcrowding our hospitals, overtaking our schools, imposing major deficits on the household market, influencing our elections, and overturning our laws. Certainly our future generations will feel this tremendous impact in significant ways.

Islamic Revolution: "Kill the infidels."

The threats that I have laid out in previous chapters are certainly causing major havoc to our way of life, and will continue if we do nothing. However, there is one emergent threat that is quickly becoming the deadliest to our faith, families, and country. It is the foremost rival to Christianity and an ideology radically opposed to the Republic of the United States of America. That threat is the Islamic Revolution.

If you spend any amount of time watching the news, you've seen the barrage of Islamic attacks happening all over the world. Hearing about terrorist plots and seeing footage of innocent civilians killed by bombers linked to terrorist groups strikes fear in Americans. To think of jihadists stopping at nothing until the flag of the crescent moon and star (symbol of the Muslim faith) flies over the White House, makes us worry about the likelihood of another major attack like September 11 on our soil.

To better understand the global threat against America, consider some of our most deadly Muslim enemies: (1) Hezbollah, (2) Hamas, (3) Muslim Brotherhood, (4) Taliban, (5) Al-Qaeda, (6) Iran, (7) Syria, (8) Pakistan, (9) Yemen, (10) Libya, and (11) Egypt. Take, for instance, groups like Hezbollah, Hamas, Taliban, Muslim Brotherhood, and Al-Qaeda. All five have something in common. They are all radical terrorist groups that seek the destruction of America and Israel. Notice how uncooperative Pakistan, Yemen and Saudi Arabia are with our government. They harbor known terrorists, fund millions of dollars to their organizations (from America), and then lie to us about having any knowledge of their terrorist activities. In the regions throughout Syria, Libya, Egypt, Iraq, and Afghanistan, continual unrest and instability weighs heavily on America's military and policies abroad.

This is the new reality we face: the majority of countries across the globe have become hostile toward America. The Arab Spring holds a fierce hatred toward the Great Satan (America) and spreads its evil all over the world. They resent American democracy and our charge to instill that in other nations. They hate America because our military presence is defilement on Arabian soil. They hate America because it has predominately been a nation of Christian beliefs. They hate America because we have been Israel's biggest supporter and defender in the Middle East.

Tolerating Ourselves to Death

Yet despite the rising danger of Islam to America, we are seeing mass attention, press, legal representation, and religious tolerance handed to Muslims across America. The liberal media love to present Islam as an oppressed religion with the need for more Americans to learn about its rich heritage. After September 11, the religious historian of the *New York Times*, Karen Armstrong, wrote an article called "The True, Peaceful Face of Islam."[14] This insidious favoritism for Islam is a developing threat to not only our national security, but to our religious freedoms as well.

The value system of tolerance espoused by liberals has allowed known terrorists (devout Muslims) the same constitutional protections we have as American citizens. For the last several years, the American Center Liberties Union (ACLU) has sponsored many conferences that promote international law in the U.S. courts. Their intent is to subvert the U.S. Constitution by allowing international law to help interpret it.

Consider this simplified example: A Muslim terrorist, while residing in America, can plot to kill thousands of American citizens, get arrested, and receive representation from the ACLU who places them under the full banner and protection of the U.S. Constitution. This is to show that Americans are to overcome our Islamophobia and respect the rights and beliefs of the Muslim faith.[15] Meanwhile, Christians are being persecuted for expressing their religious differences of the Muslim faith; Bible institutions are being sued for violating "religious freedoms;" and pastors are being threatened with lawsuits for spewing "hate crime" speech from their pulpits against Islam.

This forced tolerance of the Muslim faith is having its desired effect. It is unbelievable to think that the very freedoms we possess as American citizens are the same freedoms leveraged by Muslim terrorists to use against us. And they are doing this with the help of Americans who want to completely reform America.[16] All the while, there is an even larger agenda lurking just beneath the surface.

What is Jihad?

According to Islam, *jihad* literally means, "struggle." There are at least two primary forms of "struggle" within the teachings of Islam. The first is considered the *greater jihad* or "inner jihad" that is a *self-struggle* against sin and attempts to improve the inner qualities of self to Allah (Sura 29:68-69).[17] The theology of Islam explicitly teaches that for a Muslim to get to heaven their good deeds must outweigh their bad deeds. In Sura 42:26 it reads, "He responds with acceptance to those who believe and do good, righteous deeds...however, as to the unbelievers, for them it is severe punishment." The second is the *lesser jihad* that carries a more radical meaning of "holy war" waged on behalf of Allah. Many Islamic scholars express this to be nothing more than helping "non-Muslims" come to believe in Allah and find forgiveness in him. They do so by citing many Islamic teachings that point out that holy war is only authorized under "self-defense" or "oppression," but this explanation doesn't fully define what this truly means, thus leaving an open-ended definition and open door for active jihad (warfare).

The teachings of the Qur'an and Hadith point out that the life of a Muslim is to wage war with the enemy in an effort to balance the greater and lesser jihads in Islam, as well as to fulfill all forms of *jihad*. In order to achieve the greater jihad, the lesser jihad must be pursued and fulfilled to bring balance to Islam. However, the lesser jihad carries more meaning than simply "helping" others see the light of Islam. The Qur'an is very explicit in Sura 2:190-193, "Fight in the cause of God those who fight you ... And slay them wherever ye catch them ... And fight them on until there is no more tumult or oppression and there prevail justice and faith in God..." The Hadith 1:35 reads:

The Prophet said, 'The person who participates in (Holy battles) in Allah's cause and nothing compels him to do so except belief in Allah and His Apostles, will be recompensed by Allah either with a reward, or booty (if he survives) or will be admitted to Paradise (if he is killed in the battle as a martyr). Had I not found it difficult for my followers, then I would not remain behind any *sariya* going for Jihad and I would have loved to be martyred in Allah's cause and then made alive, and then martyred and then made alive, and then again martyred in His cause.'

The Three Jihads of History

If Americans took an honest look at the 1,400 years of violence under Islamic history, they would come to a reasonable conclusion that Islam's goal is to conquer the world by raging active jihad on all Christians, Jews and other infidels. Consider some of the following key Islamic battles:

(1) *The Arabian Jihad (622-750 AD)* – Muhammad and his followers raged war and subdued the people in the Arabian Peninsula. Upon Muhammad's death in A.D. 632, four Caliphs (Abu Bakr, Umar, Uthman, and Ali) took power and unleashed a torrent of violence, conquering the Middle East, Africa, Asia and Europe.

(2) *The Turkish Jihad (1071-1683 AD)* – The rise of the Ottoman Empire fought against Roman Catholics and Christians, beheaded many of its enemies, raped women, and enslaved non-Muslims under dhimma.

(3) *The Present Jihad* – The final battle to dominate the world and implement Sharia Law (code of law from the Qur'an).

We don't have to become experts in Islam to know the real meaning of jihad. Muhammad, the Qur'an, and the Hadith make it crystal clear that the real struggle of Islam is to kill off all who oppose Allah (Hadith 52.42; Sura 9:5). Thus, we have an overwhelming picture that the "struggles" of Islam are for Muslims to submit to Allah's will in hopes of receiving eternal salvation, and to annihilate anything in opposition to the Islamic cause.

The Eradication of the Jews

There is an old Arabic slogan, "Khaybar, Khaybar. Oh, Jews, remember. The armies of Muslims are returning." This harkens back to A.D. 629 when Muhammad and his armies invaded the oasis of Khaybar and ransacked the Jews, murdered women and children, and took the remaining Jews as slaves. This slogan has rematerialized as a call for Muslims all over the world to end the battle against the Jews once and for all. One of the last things that the Messenger of Allah said to his followers, "May Allah fight the Jews and the Christians. They took the graves of their Prophets as places of prostration. Two [religions] shall not co-exist in the land of the Arabs (Malik's Muwatta, 45:5:17)."

Where did such hatred and deadly killing among the Jews and Muslims come from? Undoubtedly, throughout the expansive history between the Jews and the Muslims, this has been highly debated. Many American Presidents have tried to bring peace to this volatile region, but the reality is this battle between the Jew and Muslim is far deeper than Americans fully grasp, let alone can solve. At the core of this raging battle for supremacy, the Muslims fight for *Arab Nationalism* (the return and reign of *Caliphate*), while the Jews fight for an *Israeli Zionism* (the return and reign of *Messiah*). If we look at the two meanings, we find that *Israel* means "struggle with God," and the word *Muslim* means "submission to Allah." In essence, from the birth of Ishmael (Gen. 16:1-16) and Isaac (Gen. 21:1-34), there was immediate conflict between the two brothers, and it has been passed down amongst their descendants (*Isaac* = Israel; *Ishmael* = Arab Nations) for the past 4,000 years!

This explains why in many Muslim schools in America, Israel has been completely removed from the world-map hanging on classroom walls. Young Muslims are taught that it's the will of Allah to eradicate Israel from the map so that they can have dominance and supremacy over the rest of the world. In the end, we know the promise God gave Abraham — that He will bless those who stand with Israel, and curse those who reject them (Gen. 12:3).

The Plan to Take Over America

In the comfort of our own homes, removed from the atrocities of the Middle East, it is easy to question the validity of the Islamic Revolution and the threat it poses to America. It is easy to brush off the alarms being sounded on talk shows and chalk it up to sensationalism. But the reality is, whether or not we acknowledge it, there is a serious strategy for our country's takeover.

Some astonishing facts came to the surface when, David Gaubatz (Special Agent with U.S. Air Force Office of Special Investigations) conducted an undercover counterintelligence operation with his son, Chris Gaubatz, who worked as an intern at the headquarters of the Council of American-Islamic Relations (CAIR) in Washington D.C. In their investigation, Gaubatz's team gained access to thousands of sensitive documents that uncovered stunning allegations that CAIR, appearing to promote peace among Americans and Muslims, was actually covertly working with the Muslim Brotherhood (a radical jihadist group funded by wealthy Saudis and Emirates in Egypt) to undermine our

U.S. Constitution and finally eliminate America.

Shockingly, they uncovered plans showing how the Muslim Brotherhood is infiltrating the United States of America and aiming to replace our U.S. Constitution with Sharia Law. Both Gaubatz and Sperry list five phases they and several other investigators believe the Muslim Brotherhood is currently executing in our country.[18]

> *Phase I:* Establishing an elite Muslim leadership while raising *taqwa*, or Islamic consciousness, in the Muslim community.
>
> *Phase II:* Creating Islamic institutions the leadership can control, along with forming autonomous Muslim enclaves.
>
> *Phase III:* Infiltrating and Islamizing America's political, social, economic, and educational systems, forming a shadow state within the state. Escalating religious conversions to Islam, manipulating mass media, and sanitizing xenophobic attacks offensive to Muslims.
>
> *Phase IV:* Publicly confronting with obvious hostility about U.S. policies, including rioting and demanding special rights and accommodations for Muslims.
>
> *Phase V:* Ultimately, a final conflict and overthrow (jihad).

If we take the 1,500 mosques (and counting), and add the millions of Muslims in America today being influenced by the radical infiltration of Wahhabism taught in hundreds of mosques and Madrassas (Islamic schools), where will this lead? The answer: to an entirely new generation of Muslims born and bred in America trained in how to take over America.[19] This growing population of American-Muslims will see to it that phases four and five will come about in their lifetime. Their strategy will include advancing hate crime speech, running for political office, producing favorable material on Islam, producing more babies than Americans, rioting for Sharia Law, and launching an all-out terrorist attack in America.[20]

Sadly, I wish we were seeing a downturn of the Islamic Revolution, but truthfully, it is only the beginning. History is plagued with events that show the utter destruction that comes from ideological revolutions. When one harkens back to Communism and Nazism confronted by FDR and Winston Churchill, history reveals the devastation and total destruction it had on most of the world. According to many experts, the Islamic Revolution is on course to potentially becoming even more destructive. The Islamic Revolution that is currently sweeping the globe comes from an ancient background. Its origin and religious roots are deeply built upon a fundamental ideology that one day the arrival of the Imam Mahdi (Guided One) will come and unleash a massive wave of warfare on the world as Islamic expansion reaches new heights.[21]

Unlike Communism and Nazism, American and European Islam masquerades as a peaceful religion as it integrates into foreign countries. However, as we've seen, this is nothing but a tactful ploy to manipulate and take control of their enemy.[22] Unknown to most Americans, the tactical phases listed by Gaubatz and Sperry are a progressive reality in our country today. They believe that the Islamic Revolution is currently at phase three of the five-step plan to eradicate America.

Stop and consider how this progressive revolution is taking shape in various schemes. Not only are there more Muslims living in the United States than Jews, but there are also tens of millions of Muslims living in both Central and South America. Intelligence now shows that Al-Qaeda and Hezbollah are coordinating with Latin America, plotting with the drug cartel and building routes to smuggle in drugs, counterfeit currency and enriched uranium into the United States. In addition, the undisclosed number of sleeper cells living in our neighborhoods will one day be activated and detonate dirty bombs in communities and high traffic areas all throughout our country.

Muslim Militancy vs. Military Might

I am absolutely convinced that the more secular and naïve our nation becomes, the easier it will be for Muslims to move in and declare America an Islamic State. We need to awaken people to the reality that without a strong and thriving military, the United States would be completely incapable of defending liberty and justice. Brad Miner asserts, "Destroy faith, demean patriotism, eviscerate conservatism, wreck capitalism, and still a semblance of America will endure—probably to rise up and correct the errors. But succeed in making us all into pacifists and in disarming our soldiers. Sailors, airmen, and Marines, and we will be lost without hope of recovery."[23]

Faced with a swelling Muslim militancy, our military is spread too thin to combat it. With the dismal plan in Afghanistan, horrific pull out in Iraq, growing unsettledness throughout the Middle East, Iran becoming a nuclear power, and major slashes to the defense budget, it will not be long until our military will be powerless to protect and defend its homeland. Bolstering the military is vital to securing our borders, protecting our interests and ensuring the survival of the American people. However, the truth is it will take much more than a governmental system and military presence in the Middle East to counter the Islamic Revolution that operates from an ideology that believes Allah wills their cause and will not stop until the caliphate (global Islamic State) has taken over the world.

The once staunch allies of America are now turning their backs in fear of the *fatwa* (religious decree) of Islam. Anticipating terrorist attacks on their lands is causing mass hysteria and destruction; something neither they nor we want to see happen in their own countries. Consequently, America will have to fight this war on terror alone, while managing to somehow maintain peace around the rest of the world.

As people around the world continue to watch the unsettledness of other nations, the following question is often asked: Is America really good for the world? Unfortunately, I believe this question is improperly posed. The question is not *if* America is good for the rest of the world, but can you imagine the world *without* America? Consider, for instance, the values and freedoms of other countries and compare how they align with America. If you were to take the liberties and opportunities that America provides immigrants, and the sacrifice and commitment that our Founders and others have made to keep America strong, you would not find another place like it in the world. This is not to say that America has remained blameless in its participation of wars, or mishandling of slavery and the killing of innocent Native Americans. But America has always resolved to improve its moral character and standards, and has remained steadfast in its efforts to make the world a safer and better place.

Think about it. Why do other nations turn to America for assistance? Why do presidents, prime ministers, and nation leaders seek counsel and resolutions from our government? The reason is simple. America is the freest, strongest and most prosperous nation on the planet. We got here because America was built on biblical principles given by God for the commonwealth of mankind. Our value system and the plentiful resources blessed by God are ways to provide assistance and protect the weak. When you track history, you will inevitably find America coming to the rescue of numerous countries, providing financial assistance, medical relief, and military power and protection against dictators who declare genocide on their own people.

The truth is without America the world would be far worse. Without America, the Arab Spring will wipe out Israel and plunder other nations in pursuit of a worldwide caliphate. The rise of terrorism will be catastrophic, sending a wave of extremists all over the world, killing infidels in the name of Allah.

Jesus said, "To whom much is given, much is required (Luke 12:48)." America has an obligation to its own people, to Israel, as well as to the rest of the world. To sit around and do nothing will signal to our enemies that it's open season. If America no longer prevents evil, it will soon enough be assimilated into the axis of evil that will replicate its destructive ways and consume the world.

CHAPTER 15

Taking Back Our Country

*"Proclaim liberty throughout the land
to all its inhabitants."*
Leviticus 25:10

[Inscription on the Liberty Bell in Philadelphia]

The growing unrest felt by many Americans is not merely due to the economic turbulence, but mainly to the spiritual unrest that is costing us more than just untold sums of money. [1]

Jesus said, "What profits a man if he loses his soul and gains the whole world (Mk. 8:36)?" According to Jesus, we can pursue all the riches in the world and still be left with nothing. This is why the nation as a whole is shifting away from the moral standards of God because it is more captivated by the illustrious desires of the flesh over pursuing and enjoying the freedom found in Christ.

Our greedy indulgences will overcome us unless we willingly admit the need for Christ and choose to live righteously in accordance to the Word of God (Ps. 25:8). This final chapter will inspire you (the Christian) to fight to preserve the U.S. Constitution, get involved in downsizing BIG GOV'T and addressing the danger of the Islamic Revolution. It is my hope that you take this material and expand its truths in your life and family, so that together, we can and will take back our country and preserve its costly freedoms for our children's children!

Preserve the U.S. Constitution

According to the U.S. Constitution, the size and scope of government was never meant to be an intrusive and abusive form of centralized power, but a philosophy of delegated and enumerated powers with checks and balances. The Framers' sensitivity to outside exploitation of the government was the reason for constructing a three-branch system of government that monitors and holds each other accountable under the guise, support and approval of the American people, not through culturally corrupt persuasion.

From our country's founding documents: Declaration of Independence, U.S. Constitution and Bill of Rights come the establishment, role and purpose government has in our society. Listed below is a constitutional overview of the role of government using these three primary sources.

1. The government is not to have power over the people, but people over the government.
2. The government is instituted among people and receives its allotted role to serve and protect them.
3. The government is to preserve the unalienable rights of the people.
4. The government is to submit to the power of the people if they see the right to dissolve or abolish it and institute new government.
5. The government is not to legislate arbitrary or capricious laws, but only laws that the governed consent.
6. The government is to enact justice.
7. The government is to regulate commerce between the states and maintain a strong currency.
8. The government is to protect the life, liberty and property of the people from threats within and abroad.

Our country faces a serious dilemma: remain an ordered society or relinquish its freedom. President Ronald Reagan said, "Freedom is never more than one generation away from extinction. We didn't pass it to our children in the bloodstream. It must be fought for, protected, and handed on for them to do the same, or one day we will spend our sunset years telling our children and our children's children what it was once like in the United States where men were free."[2]

The truth is Congress is not authorized to *prevent* students from gathering in prayer at school, or preclude sporting events from writing Bible verses on jerseys or banners, or expel students for bringing their Bibles to class. Rather, it's the role of Congress to *protect* students' and teachers' religious rights under their First Amendment rights. The moment BIG GOV'T privatizes faith from public life, they are enforcing upon our civility a secularized version of legislative powers. As Christians, we are not called to be *subordinate* to BIG GOV'T, but *submissive* to God (Ac. 4:19, 20; 5:29)! We are not to be *anti-government*, but unequivocally *anti-tyranny*. That is why we will not bend our values nor compromise our beliefs, but will stand for the self-governance of each and every American within the limitations and parameters of the government (Rom. 13).

True connection between private morality and public policy are two "indissoluble unions" that make for a better life for all Americans. This is why churches and families all across this land need to go out in full force to educate more of their congregants and friends with the facts in this book and work together in ending the threats that seek to destroy the U.S. Constitution. One way to do this is if more people got their churches to organize training events in their communities that teach the truth behind American history and the real freedom and protections we have under the U.S. Constitution.[3]

Build a Legacy of Hard Work

Despair, greed and hopelessness are not what we want to pass on to the next generation. If we are going to get out of the bondage of debt and begin to prosper, then we need to repent of our greed and turn back to God like the Hebrews did while enslaved in Egypt (Exodus 3:7-10). The kind of real change our children need to see is homes displaying thankful hearts for the many blessings and provisions of God. Moses warned Israel, "When you have eaten and are satisfied, praise the Lord your God for the good land He has given you. Be careful that you do not forget the Lord your God, failing to observe His commands, His laws and His decrees (Deut. 8:10, 11)." Our homes need to have trust and great humility in God (Ps. 28:7) and a generous heart to give to help the poor and needy (Rom. 15:26; 2 Cor. 9:6-11; Gal. 2:10).

We need to model for the next generation that hard work and ingenuity brings out the best and brightest in us. We need to teach our children not to be lazy, but demonstrate that hard work is the driving force that earns the rewards that comes from honest work (Eph. 4:28; 1 Thess. 4:11). The Bible puts it plainly, "All hard work brings a profit, but mere talk leads only to poverty (Pro. 14:23)." Children need to see what a life of hard works looks like and the benefits that comes from hard work. We need to be good stewards of the gifts, talents and financial resources given as a loan by God. And may we never rely on government handouts, but always strive to earn a living that honors God, provides for our families and builds up the economy of the United States of America!

Families need to make *wiser* decisions to live a debt free life, not *wishful* thinking that leads to a debt-burdened life. There is great urgency to start practicing conservative principles in the way we make, spend and manage money.[4] This is a foreign concept because many measure success and good parenting based on the things they possess and give their children. But the real value is in teaching children to live a virtuous life that puts the needs of people above the desire for more things (Lk. 12:13-34). The next generation must learn that true prosperity never comes from self-individualism, but self-discipline that trumps greed and failure. Once Christian Americans get their family house in order individually, they will enlarge their understanding of getting their house in order nationally.

Produce a Strong National Economy

When you talk to the average American, they would say that it's common sense not to spend what you don't have, and yet, BIG GOV'T continues to increase spending. Jesus reminded, "For where your treasure is, there your heart will be also (Matt. 6:21)." We can easily find America's heart turned to the pleasures of money and obsessed with what it can buy. However, this is problematic because our selfish pleasures and illustrious desires only bring debt and destruction. As Solomon said, "Trust in your money and down you go (Proverbs 11:28)."

My reason for addressing this often-neglected issue in Christian discourse is because it plays a huge role in shaping our society, families and way of living. The state of our economy and country has great impact on family. What more is required before we fully realize the danger we are in as a nation if we go completely bankrupt?

We have an opportunity for a better future if Christians simply wake up and take these steps to save our country from economic ruin.

The first step to save our country is to stop wasteful spending by the superfluity of BIG GOV'T. Rather than help small businesses produce more jobs and stimulate the economy, BIG GOV'T inevitably increases the deficit at alarming rates, takes over the common sector, and becomes the majority investor in the economic activity of America. If we want to get our country out of debt and produce a stronger economy, then we must follow the action plan below.

1. Stop borrowing and printing money.
2. Reduce the level of spending each year by over 20% of the gross domestic product (GDP).
3. Pay down interest payments to reduce the rate and keep inflation down.
4. Prevent the debt ceiling to be raised every year.
5. Increase the value of our currency and strengthen the dollar.
6. Simplify the tax code and save American families $100 billion a year.

MONETARY ECONOMY *"We the People"*	REGULATORY ECONOMY *"We the GOV'T"*
Maintains GDP	*Manipulates* GDP
Monitors Balance Sheets	*Enlarges* Balance Sheets
Reserves Profits	*Eliminates* Profits
Determined by Businesses	*Controlled* by Fed
Decreases Inflation	*Increases* Inflation

The second step to save our country is to cut federal and corporate taxes and give incentives to create more jobs in America.[5]

The third step to save our country is to stop relying on foreign oil. We need to dismantle the EPA and create oil-producing jobs that will provide more energy and sustainability long term. As Christians, it is our moral responsibility to practice effective stewardship that protects and maintains conservation. We don't have to jeopardize human life to protect rare animal species or limited natural resources.

Listed below are four practical points I believe (as a Christian) will prosper America without harming our environment.

1. Energy producers need to stop looking for government subsidies and start being cost competitive. This would remove BIG GOV'T from the private sector and allow innovators to thrive.
2. Once the political and special interest groups are out of the energy market, America can return to producing affordable energy by using the savings from tax cuts.
3. States that are the most oil-rich, such as New Mexico, North Dakota, California, Alaska, and Texas, ought to set the standard of exploring, drilling, producing, and selling reliable energy across state lines at an affordable cost. States should collaborate with oil companies and work together to hire independent scientists to help explore, produce, and conserve oil. Each state has the sovereign right to manage and operate their plants and services, not the EPA.
4. Let's generate the right programs and incentives so the next generation can be a part of new energy innovation and technology at home and abroad.[6]

Protect Our Borders

There is no simple solution to the immigration problem. This is a volatile issue and certainly an emotional one because of the personal ties most people have to immigration. But the fact remains that almost all developed countries in the world have immigration laws and have governments in place to pass judgment on crimes committed by those who break such laws. Illegal immigration is not a matter of segregation, but about national security and human decency. That means it is important to enforce laws that keep our own citizens safe while ensuring the respect of all human beings in the process.

The Bible makes a clear case that we are to respect the "foreigner" or "alien" among us (Ex. 12:49). But in context of Scripture (Ex. 12:48; Lev. 19:33-34; 24:22; Nu. 15:15-16), the foreigner must comply with the laws and ordinances of the foreign nation in order to access such privileges. Immigration is not about fairness; more importantly it's about following and obeying the law of the land (Rom. 13; Tit. 3:1; 1 Pet. 2:13-17). As Christians, we need to make sure that we follow and obey the laws, but also ensure that the enforced legislation is theologically and humanely sound.[7]

The truth is it's going to take more than amnesty and labor unions to solve this crisis. The short list below is only a portion of what it will take to turn our immigration problem around. I realize there are more solutions beyond what's offered here, but what will truly make a difference is churches (and individual Christians) rolling up their sleeves and getting more involved.

1. We need to treat each person (whether legal or illegal) with mutual respect and with a desire to help improve his or her situation. We are all aliens and sojourners in this world. As Christians (particularly), our true citizenship is in heaven (Phil. 3:20), not America. We certainly need to make better progress in protecting our freedoms, but to do so with a heavenly perspective, and not just a temporal one (Col. 3:1-3; 1 Pet. 1:1).

2. We need immigration reform to improve the U.S Citizenship and Immigration Services and apply the law more practically to legalize the immigrants who have suffered long delays. We need to crack down on those who pose a threat, not penalize those who obey the law.

3. We need to work with both the federal and state

governments and law enforcements to fund enough money to patrol and control our borders and coast-lines. (While I'm in favor of funding our borders, we also need to look at negotiable incentives with Canada, Mexico and Central America to cooperate with our plans and strategies to enforce our immigration laws. We must get them to comply with our laws, but we must do it in a way that maintains a dignified approach to assimilating immigrants in our country and appreciating their contributions as well).[8]

4. We need more immigration centers in key places, such as Latin America, Central America, and Asia, so foreigners can apply for a work visa, find a job and coordinate with banks and credit card companies to track work visa holders.

5. We must withhold certain benefits to Mexico until they are willing to help solve the problem of illegal immigration within their own country.

6. We should actively support and praise those politicians and legislatures who are enforcing the law and cracking down on companies hiring illegals. Every time a business owner hires an illegal off the books, that owner is conducting illegal business and stifling the opportunity for hard working Americans to work legally! Corporations participating in these activities need to be penalized to the full extent of the law.

7. We need to enforce more immigration laws whereby the states have the right to process illegal aliens and reward those who obey the laws.

8. We need to get more members of Congress partnering with churches to provide more ESL and U.S. citizenship classes for immigrants.

Encounter the Muslim World

It's very troubling to think that America is progressively exchanging the teachings of Jesus, "Love your neighbor (Mk. 12:31)" for a much more radical teaching of Muhammad that orders, "Fight everyone in the way of Allah and kill those who disbelieve in Allah (Ibn Ishaq 992)."

We can no longer supplement the teachings of Jesus for a spirit of tolerance and acceptance of a "peaceful" religion that seeks no harm. The Islamic Revolution involves much more than a few extremists wearing masks, strapping explosives on themselves, and yelling "Allahu Akbar" (Allah is the Greatest) before they kill innocent people. While there are many good and law-abiding Muslims in America, there's still a large Muslim population supportive of the September 11 attacks and committed to active jihad.

Hopefully, after reading about the Islamic Revolution, you've come to see that the core of Islam is not for peace. Consider the violence that is spelled out directly in the religious writings of Islam, espoused by Muslim leaders, and perpetrated by its followers. The fact remains Islam is an ancient religion embedded in violence and holds to a violent future as well.

Christians need to take the Islamic Revolution seriously and stand up to prevent Muslims from taking over our country and Christian heritage. If Christians don't take this threat seriously and defend the Christian faith, I believe the Muslim faith will eventually be the controlling religion in America. I encourage every Christian to be equipped with a biblical worldview, and stay informed of the dangers of Islam.[9] We need to not only be on the defensive (against the attacks of Islam), but on the offensive (mobilize trained Christians to advance the truth of Christianity) in the mainstream once again. As Edmund Burke stated, "All that is necessary for evil to triumph is for good men to do nothing."[10]

Jesus Christ	Muhammad	
Never Murdered	Murdered Thousands	Medina, A.D. 627
Never Owned Slaves	Took Slaves After Battles; Including Women	Sura 8:41; Conquest of Khaybar, A.D. 628
Never Forced Belief	Forced Allegiance or Threatened Death	Hadith (al-Bukhari), Vol. 9, Bk. 84, No. 57
Performed Miracles	Performed No Miracles	Suras 29:51; 3:181-184
Sacrificed His Own Life	Sacrificed the Lives of Others	Beat Wives: Sura 4:34 Cut off Hands of Thieves: Sura 5:38 Assassinations: Suras 3:186; 33:57 Martyrdom: Sura 44:51-56 Violent Crusades: Sura 9:29
Offered Salvation	No Assurance of Salvation	Sura 46:9

A CALL TO ACTION

A s you read this book, I pray that you were not only awakened to the threats but also recharged to be a beacon of light in the midst of the darkness permeating the world. Jesus said, "You are the light of the world. A city on a hill cannot be hidden (Matt. 5:14)." Paul expressed the confidence that Christians are to be "blameless and pure, children of God without fault in a crooked and depraved generation, in which you shine like stars in the universe (Phil. 2:15)." The single greatest obstacle for Christians is not the inability to defend the faith (though that is lacking), but whether or not they will faithfully live out their faith and change the world!

According to the Olivet Discourse (Matt. 24-25; Mk.13; Lk. 21), Jesus prophesied that the world would continue to grow darker as the end drew nearer. He warned, "Nation will rise against nation, and kingdom against kingdom (Matt. 24:7)." Jesus predicted that His followers would experience intense persecutions, and for some, even death (Matt. 24:9). Paul vigorously wrote that there "will be terrible times in the last days (2 Tim. 3:1)," and in the "last times some will turn away from the true faith; they will follow deceptive spirits and teachings that come from demons (1 Tim. 4:1)." Peter reminded his readers in the midst of intense persecution that in the "last days scoffers will come, mocking the truth and following their own desires (2 Pet. 3:3)." In light of this, it should come as no surprise to Christians how things are progressively getting worse as the end draws nearer.

Nevertheless, that does not mean that you carry a "gloom-and-doom" forecast of the world wherever you go. The truth is no man knows the day or the hour of Christ's return or how much time is left (Matt. 24:36). Therefore, as long as you are alive in this world, you are to shine brightly and penetrate the darkness, not to be overcome by it (1 Pet. 1:14). Jesus told Nicodemus, "This is the verdict: Light has come into the world, but men loved darkness instead of light because their deeds were evil. Everyone who does evil hates the light, and will not come into the light for fear that his deeds will be exposed. But whoever lives by the truth comes into the light, so that it may be seen plainly that what he has done has been done through God (Jn. 3:19-21)." As you live by the truth of God's Word, you are making the light shine brighter in this corrupt world. May those around you be able to see plainly what God has done through you, and from that, come to know the truth of Christ.

God has not called you to conform to the world, but instead, to be transformed by His perfect will (Rom. 12:2). He has called you not to be ashamed of the gospel of Christ, but to speak boldly His truth as a faithful witness of Christ (Rom. 1:16; 2 Cor. 5:20)! This is what those who are lost and blinded need to hear in order to come to a saving knowledge of Jesus Christ. God sends messengers to preach the gospel, just like Christ went to visit Nicodemus.

Jesus tells the story of a master who puts a certain servant in charge over his other servants. Either he will be faithful to the call of his master or not (Matt. 24:45-51). The same applies to you. Jesus has put you in charge of certain responsibilities, and when He returns, will He find favor in you? Will you be faithful with what He has given you?

In another parable Jesus tells the story of a master

giving a portion of talents to each servant. Upon his return, the master found that two of his servants brought profitability to his investment (Matt. 25:14-23). Unfortunately the other servant had buried his talent, producing nothing (25:24-25). The master responded saying, "You wicked, lazy servant! So you knew that I harvest where I have not sown and gather where I have not scattered seed (25:26)?" What is the meaning of this parable? Jesus has given you (as a Christian), a certain gift and talent that is to be invested for a greater return. So the question you need to answer is whether or not you are investing your gifts and reaping profits for God?

If you feel that you have been a "lazy" servant, take heart that God forgives you and desires to use you to advance His Kingdom here on earth. Here are a few points to help you, a servant of the Lord, invest your gifts and reap an abundance for Him.

As a Christian, you need to daily consecrate yourself before God.

Each day make it your aim to consecrate yourself before a holy and living God (Lev. 11:44). The psalmist shouts, "Rejoice in the Lord, you who are righteous, and praise His holy name (97:12). The more diligent you are in being set apart for God's work in your life, the greater impact you will have on those around you.

As a Christian, you need to pray and intercede for America and its national leaders.

It is vital that you set a portion of time aside each day and lift up the needs of your country, and pray for the salvation, safety and godly wisdom for the elected officials and military of America (1 Tim. 2:1-2). If America has any fighting chance of being restored, it is going to take a massive number of Christians turning from their apathy and self-dependence and praying for the restoration of their nation. Simply put, a restored republic is one that humbles itself before the mercies of God, and submits its will to the King of Kings and Lord of Lords. King David declared, "All the ends of the earth will remember and turn to the Lord, and all the families of the nations will bow down before Him, for dominion belongs to the Lord and He rules over the nations (Ps. 22:27-28)."

As a Christian, you need to mature in your faith and extend it to your surrounding influences.

You read in chapter two how many Christians are biblically illiterate due in large part because they are either too busy to read the Bible, or simply find it too difficult to understand. Let that not be true of you! Make time to read and study the Bible everyday. In these times of studying the Bible, you will sharpen your faith, build your trust in God, and be given the counsel and wisdom needed everyday to make wise choices. The Bible promises you that if you grow in your faith, you will not be "ineffective and unproductive in your knowledge of our Lord Jesus Christ (2 Pet. 1:8)." On the contrary, you will be a mature Christian who is adequate to teach and disciple others (2 Tim. 2:1-2; 3:16-17). That is precisely the command that Jesus Christ gave His followers prior to His ascension. He said, "Make disciples of all nations (Matt. 28:19)."

Just think what impact this would have on your family, co-workers, neighbors, and the rest of the world if you simply matured in your faith and made an effort to disciple others according to the teachings of Jesus? So here's my closing point to you: *study the Bible and teach the Bible*. Don't settle for anything less!

As a Christian, you need to get and stay involved in issues that impact your family and the society you live in.

Hopefully you not only found this book to be informative, but also instructive in helping you connect the dots to a bigger picture of the state and condition of America. It is not enough for a Christian to only be concerned with issues centered around his or her own life, but to take interest in issues surrounding the world they live in as well.

If you recall, the early settlers didn't settle under the oppression of the King of England. They risked their own lives and livelihood to flee and establish a freer and more desirable place. Their action landed them in America and several years later spread into colonies, which eventually became the United States of America. (Talk about getting involved and changing the world!)

I encourage you to reexamine this book and find the issues that speak to you most and get involved. Don't just sit around and complain about all the problems and point the finger. Be a Christian who stays informed and has an active platform to inform and assemble an army of believers throughout America. You may be wondering what kind of platform you can build? That's easy. It starts with your own family. When the family is strong and proactive in the culture, it increases the health and wealth of the Christian Church and the community. When the family is growing strong in its faith in God, then the public square of ideas will reflect a more dependence on Jesus Christ. But this won't happen if you choose to do nothing.

As a Christian, you need to accept your call and minister to the needs of others.

Some of you, God has called to be teachers and preachers of His Word, while others are called to be laymen and helpers. There is not one call that is greater than the other. What is important is whether or not you are willing to submit your will and take up your cross daily and follow the Lord (Lk. 9:23).

God called me to be a pastor – to serve, teach, and disciple the body of Christ. From that, He called me to start re|shift Ministries and write this book. Just as God has called me to fight this raging war of ideas, He has called you! So whatever God is calling you to do, will you leave your comfort zone and do what is necessary for Him? Paul reminds Christians to "make the most of every opportunity, because the days are evil. Therefore, do not be foolish, but understand what the Lord's will is (Eph. 5:16-17)." Are you willing to answer His call?

God called Daniel to resist a hostile environment in Babylon, and lead a charge against its false idols and worship. Daniel didn't refuse the call of God just because he felt out of place or outnumbered. The Bible says that Daniel "resolved not to defile himself (Dan. 1:8)," but to remain faithful to God's law. His bold allegiance to God demonstrates an unrelenting desire not to compromise and give in. Daniel's God-honoring response in the midst of extreme pressure and hostility is the sort of example needed in America today.

I pray you have become awakened to a new sense of faith, hope and love and that you will stand up and join the fight to take back your faith, family and country! I must say to you, dear Christian, that it will be no easy task. But this is the mission that God has called His followers to undertake. It is going to take a revival in each Christian home, starting with you, then your spouse, and finally your entire family. It is going to take the body of Christ uniting together upon His truth and living out His Word before an unbelieving generation. It is going to take prayer and fasting, and the assembling of these godly families and leaders from various institutions to conduct open and civil discourse to restore God, truth and moral values back into America. It is my closing prayer that you glorify God in His calling on your life as you always anticipate the return of Jesus Christ!

To Him who is able to keep you from falling and to present you before His glorious presence without fault and with great joy — to the only God our Savior be glory, majesty, power and authority, through Jesus Christ our Lord, before all ages, now and forevermore! Amen.

Jude 1:24-25

ENDNOTES

CHAPTER 1: Our Christian Heritage

[1] Gary DeMar, "Christian Colonies," *American's Christian History: The Untold Story.* 2nd ed. (Powder Springs, GA: American Vision, 1995), 56.

[2] Alister McGrath, *Christianity's Dangerous Idea: The Protestant Revolution – A History from the Sixteenth Century to the Twenty-First* (New York: HarperCollins, 2007), 152.

CHAPTER 2: Threat #1: Remove God

[1] Tyndale House Publishers, *Holy Bible: New Living Translation*, 3rd ed. (Carol Stream, IL: Tyndale House, 2007), Jeremiah 7:28.

[2] Charles Colson and Nancy Pearcey, *How Now Shall We Live?* (Carol Stream, IL: Tyndale House, 1999), 22.

[3] "Is the Pledge of Allegiance Unconstitutional?" Albert Mohler, http://www.albertmohler.com/2005/09/15/is-the-pledge-of-allegiance-unconstitutional/.

[4] "God in America/God in the White House; Dwight D. Eisenhower," PBS, published October 11, 2010, http://www.pbs.org/godinamerica/god-in-the-white-house/.

5   The New Atheist movement consists of Richard Dawkins, Christopher Hitchens, Sam Harris, and Daniel Dennett.

6   A few famous proponents of naturalism: David Hume (*A Treatise on Human Nature*), Charles Darwin (*On the Origin of Species*), Karl Marx (*The Communist Manifesto*), Carl Sagan (*Cosmos*), and Richard Dawkins (The Blind Watchmaker).

7   Friedrich Nietzsche, *The Gay Science: With a Prelude in Rhymes and an Appendix of Songs*, trans. and comm. by Walter Arnold Kaufmann (New York: Random House, 1974), 181.

8   "A Bible in the Hand Still May Not be Read," Baptist Standard, accessed June 24, 2012, http://www.baptist-standard.com/2000/12_4/pages/biblereading.html.

9   Chap Clark, *Hurt 2.0: Inside the World of Today's Teenagers* (Grand Rapids: Baker Academic, 2011), Kindle edition.

CHAPTER 3: Threat #2: Redefine Truth

1   "The Colbert Report: The Word — Truthiness", Colbert Nation, http://www.colbertnation.com/the-colbert-report-videos/24039/october-17-2005/the-word—-truthiness.

2   Norman Geisler and Paul Hoffman, *Why I Am a Christian: Leading Thinkers Explain Why They Believe (Rev. and expanded ed.)* (Grand Rapids: BakerBooks, 2006), 24-25.

³   Ravi Zacharias defines absolutes as "basically an unchanging point of reference by which all other changes are measured." Ravi Zacharias, *Deliver Us From Evil*, (Nashville: W Publishing 1997), 219.

⁴   Walt Mueller, *Youth Culture 101* (Grand Rapids: Zondervan, 2007), 83-84.

⁵   Christian Smith, *Soul Searching: The Religious and Spiritual Lives of American Teenagers* (New York: Oxford University Press, 2005), 73-75.

⁶   "Pornography Statistics," Family Safe Media, http://www.familysafemedia.com/pornography_statistics.html.

⁷   Ben Shapiro, *Porn Generation: How Social Liberalism Is Corrupting Our Future* (Washington DC: Regnery, 2005), 2.

CHAPTER 4: Threat #3: Replace Christianity

¹   C. S. Lewis, *The Quotable Lewis*, ed. Wayne Martindale and Jerry Root (Wheaton, IL: Tyndale House, 1989), 177.

²   Kenneth D. Boa and Robert M. Bowman Jr., *An Unchanging Faith In A Changing World: Understanding and Responding to Critical Issues that Christians Face Today* (Nashville: Thomas Nelson, 1997), p. 170.

³   Colson and Pearcey, *How Now Shall We Live*, 22.

⁴   Alexis de Tocqueville, Henry Reeve, and John C. Spencer, *Democracy in America* (New York: Allard and Saunders, 1838), 319.

⁵   "North Carolina Constitution of 1776," Beliefnet,

http://www.beliefnet.com/resourcelib/docs/169/
North_Carolina_Constitution_of_1776_1.html.

[6]   David Barton, *The Jefferson Lies: Exposing the Myths You Always Believed About Thomas Jefferson* (Nashville: Thomas Nelson, 2012), 120.

[7]   "The Northwest Ordinance, Article III", Northwest Ordinance, http://www.northwestordinance.org/.

[8]   Jefferson was not the architect of the First Amendment (read the letter to Madison on December 20, 1787), and his letter using the phrase "wall of separation" was written over ten years after the First Amendment was ratified!

[9]   H. A. Washington, *The Writings of Thomas Jefferson: Being His Autobiography, Correspondence, Reports, Messages, Addresses, and Other Writings, Official and Private,* Pub. by the Order of the Joint Committee of Congress on the Library, from the Original Manuscripts, Deposited in the Department of State (Washington, D.C.: Taylor & Maury, 1853), 441.

[10]   "The Kentucky Resolutions of 1798," Constitution Society, last updated November 4, 2011, http://www.constitution.org/cons/kent1798.htm.

[11]   "Amendment I (Religion), Document 58, Thomas Jefferson to Danbury Baptist Association," The Founder's Constitution, http://www.presspubs.uchicago.edu/founders/documents/amendI_religions58.html.

[12]   "Amendment I (Religion), Document 60, Thomas Jefferson to Rev. Samuel Miller," The Founder's Constitution,

http://www.press-pubs.uchicago.edu/founders/documents/amendI_religions60.html.

[13] "Message from John Adams to the Officers of the First Brigade of the Third Division of the Militia of Massachusetts," Beliefnet, http://www.beliefnet.com/resourcelib/docs/115/Message_from_John_Adams_to_the_Officers_of_the_First_Brigade_1.html.

[14] Barton, *The Jefferson Lies*, 126-127.

[15] "McCollum v. Board of Education - 333 U.S. 203 (1948)," Justia US Supreme Court Center, http://www.supreme.justia.com/cases/federal/us/333/203/case.html.

[16] Matthew Spaulding, *We Still Hold These Truths: Rediscovering Our Principles, Reclaiming Our Future* (Wilmington, DE: ISI Books, 2009), 56.

[17] "Rehnquist's Dissent in Wallace v Jaffree (1985)," Belcher Foundation, http://www.belcherfoundation.org/wallace_v_jaffree_dissent.htm.

CHAPTER 5: Taking Back Our Faith

[1] A.W. Tozer, *The Attributes of God* (Camp Hill, PA: Christian Publications, 1997), 5.

[2] J. I. Packer, *Concise Theology: A Guide to Historic Christian Beliefs* (Wheaton, IL: Tyndale House, 1995), 267.

[3] Read "Pennsylvania Charter of Privileges," Historic Documents, http://www.ushistory.org/documents/charter.htm.

4   "Was George Washington a Christian?" Christian Answers, accessed August 27, 2012, http://www.christiananswers.net/q-wall/wal-g011.html.

5   James Robison and Jay W. Richards, *Indivisible: Restoring Faith, Family and Freedom Before It's Too Late* (New York: FaithWords, Hachette Group, 2012), iBooks, 108.

6   Some great biblical worldview ministries: re|shift Ministries; Ravi Zacharias International Ministries; Summit Ministries; Chuck Colson Worldview Center; Worldview Academy; Worldview Ministries; Probe Ministries; Stand to Reason.

CHAPTER 6: Family: The Heart of America!

1   "Patrick Henry Quotations," Revolutionary War and Beyond, accessed Sept. 9, 2012, http://www.revolutionary-war-and-beyond.com/patrick-henry-quotations.html.

2   "Mr. Thomas Manton's Epistle to the Reader," Center for Reformed Theology and Apologetics, http://www.reformed.org/documents/wcf_standards/index.html?mainframe=/documents/wcf_standards/p009-manton_to_the_reader.html.

3   Diane Severance, "Jonathan Edwards, America's Humble Giant," Christianity.com, accessed Aug. 29, 2012, http://www.christianity.com/ChurchHistory/11630188/page3/.

4   Richard Baxter, *The Reformed Pastor* (London: Religious Tract Society, 1862), 91.

5   See Edmund S. Morgan, *The Puritan Family: Religion*

& Domestic Relations in Seventeenth-Century New England (New York: Harper & Row, 1966).

6   Dale Taylor, *The Writer's Guide to Everyday Life in Colonial America* (Cincinnati: Writer's Digest, 1997), 120.

7   David Freeman Hawke, *Everyday Life in Early America* (New York: Harper & Row, 1988), 60.

CHAPTER 7: Threat #1: Remove Family Structure

1   "Divorce Statistics and Divorce Rate in the USA," Divorce Statistics, last modified April 5, 2012, http://www.divorcestatistics.info/divorce-statistics-and-divorce-rate-in-the-usa.html.

2   John MacArthur, *The Fulfilled Family: God's Design for Your Home*, 15-16 of 201, iBooks.

3   U.S. Department of Commerce, Economics and Statistics Administration, Children's Living Arrangements and Characteristics by Jason Fields, Washington DC: U.S. Census Bureau, 2003.

4   Steven L. Nock and Christopher J. Einolf, "The One Hundred Billion Dollar Man: The Annual Public Costs of Father Absence," National Fatherhood Initiative, accessed May 23, 2012, http://www.fatherhood.org/media/fatherhood-statistics/one-hundred-billion-dollar-man-download.

5   Frank I. Luntz, "I Can See Clearly Now," Chap. 1, *What Americans Really Want...Really: The Truth about Our Hopes, Dreams, and Fears* (New York: Hyperion, 2009).

[6] Norman L. Geisler and Peter Bocchino, *Unshakable Foundations* (Minneapolis: Bethany House, 2001), 207.

[7] Paul Leicester Ford, *The New England Primer: A History of Its Origin and Development with a Reprint of the Unique Copy of the Earliest Known Edition and Many Facsimile Illustrations and Reproductions* (New York: Teachers College, Columbia University, 1962).

[8] Henry Steele Commager (ed.), "Massachusetts School Law of 1647," *Documents of American History* (New York: F. S. Crofts, 1947), 29. Also in Ellwood P. Cubberley (ed.), *Readings in the History of Education* (Boston: Houghton Mifflin, 1920), 299.

[9] Benjamin Franklin, *The Papers of Benjamin Franklin*, Leonard W. Labaree (ed.) (New Haven: Yale University Press, 1961) vol. III, p. 413; "Proposals Relating to the Education of Youth in Pennsylvania," 1749.

[10] Larry Schweikart, *What Would the Founders Say? A Patriot's Answers to America's Most Pressing Problems* (New York: Sentinel, 2011), 256.

[11] Vidal v. Girard's Executors, 43 U.S 153, 171 (1844).

[12] "Thomas Henry Huxley (1825-1895)," Internet Encyclopedia of Philosophy, accessed August 30, 2012, http:/www.iep.utm.edu/huxley/.

[13] "Herbert Spencer (1820-1903)," Internet Encyclopedia of Philosophy, accessed August 30, 2012, http://www.iep.utm.edu/spencer/.

[14] See "Ten Major Court Cases about Evolution and

Creationism," NCSE, last modified July 30, 2007, http://www.ncse.com/taking-action/ten-major-court-cases-evolution-creationism.

[15] Julian Huxley, "At Random," a television preview on Nov. 21, 1959. Also, Sol Tax, *Evolution of Life* (Chicago: University Press, 1960), 1.

[16] "Thirty Enumerated Powers," Tenth Amendment Center, accessed Sept. 5, 2012, http://www.tenthamendmentcenter.com/historical-documents/united-states-constitution/thirty-enumerated-powers/.

[17] William J. Bennett, *America: The Last Best Hope – Vol. 1: From the Age of Discovery to a World of War* (Nashville: Nelson Current, 2006), 110.

[18] For more information about the history of the Department of Education, read *Department of Education: Timeline of Growth* by Chris Edwards http://www.downsizinggovernment.org/education/timeline.

[19] For information on Teachers' Unions: http://www.teachersunionexposed.com/

[20] G. Gregory Moo, *Power Grab: How the National Education Association Is Betraying Our Children* (Washington, DC: Regnery, 1999), 222.

[21] Moo, *Power Grab*, 337.

[22] Lindsey Burke, "NEA Convention Reminds Us: It's About Union Power, Not Children," The Foundry: Conservative Policy News Blog from The Heritage Foundation, published July 2, 2011, http://www.blog.

heritage.org/2011/07/02/nea-convention-reminds-us-it's-about-union-power-not-children/.

[23] "Protecting Children by Empowering Parents," ParentalRights.org, accessed Aug. 30, 2012. http://www. parentalrights.org/index.asp?Type=B_BASIC.

[24] "Convention on the Rights of the Child," Office of the United Nations High Commissioner for Human Rights, accessed Sept. 9, 2012, http://www2.ohchr.org/english/law/crc.htm.

[25] Archibald Alexander Hodge, *Popular Lectures on Theological Themes* (Philadelphia: Presbyterian Board of Publication, 1887), 281-83.

[26] Robert P. George and Melissa Moschella, "Does Sex Ed Undermine Parental Rights?" The New York Times, published October 18, 2011, http://www.nytimes. com/2011/10/19/opinion/does-sex-ed-undermine-parental-rights.html?_r=2.

[27] "NEA to UN: More Graphic Sex-Ed Needed," ParentalRights.org, http://www.parentalrights.org/index. asp?Type=B_BASIC&SEC=%7BEC9944B8-96D9-4581-A9AE-06DD3173C964%7D.

[28] Chad Hills, "NYC's Mandated Violation of Innocence," CitizenLink, last modified August 19 2011, http://www. citizenlink.com/2011/08/19/nyc's-mandated-violation-of-innocence/.

[29] Berit Kjos, "Brainwashing in America: Why Few Dare Call It Conspiracy," last modified 2001, http://www.cross-road.to/articles2/brainwashing.html.

[30] Dan Lips, Shanea Watkins and John Fleming, "Does Spending More on Education Improve Academic Achievement?" Heritage Foundation, last modified September 8, 2008, http://www.heritage.org/research/reports/2008/09/does-spending-more-on-education-improve-academic-achievement?query=does+spending+m ore+on+education+improve+academic+achievement.

[31] Dennis Prager, *Still the Best Hope: Why the World Needs American Values to Triumph* (New York: Harper Collins) Kindle edition, 472-475.

[32] "High School Reform," Education Week, published August 4, 2004, http://www.edweek.org/ew/issues/high-school-reform/.

[33] "Indicators of School Crime and Safety," NCES Bureau of Justice Statistics, http://www.nces.ed.gov/pubs2012/2012002.pdf.

[34] "Addiction: A Preventable and Treatable Disease", CASA Columbia, 2012, http://www.casacolumbia.org/articlefiles/687-20120712annualreport2011.pdf.

[35] "2010 National Teen Survey Finds: More Than One Quarter of Public School Students Attend Gang-and Drug-Infected Schools," PR Newswire, published Aug. 19, 2012, http://www.prnewswire.com/news-releases/2010-national-teen-survey-finds-more-than-one-quarter-of-public-school-students-attend-gang — and-drug-infected-schools-101045204.html.

[36] Carl Azuz, "Survey: 17% of High Schoolers Drink, Smoke, Use Drugs during School Day," CNN Schools of Thought Blog, published August 22, 2012. http://www.

schoolsofthought.blogs.cnn.com/2012/08/22/survey-17-of-high-schoolers-drink-smoke-use-drugs-during-school-day/.

[37] See Christopher J. Klicka, "Decisions of the United States Supreme Court Upholding Parental Rights as 'Fundamental,'" HSLDA, published October 27, 2003, http://www.hslda.org/docs/nche/000000/00000075.asp.

[38] Sign the Parental Rights Amendment and support it into legislation across the country (www.parentalrights.org).

[39] See "Key Facts: The Need to Protect Parental Rights," True Tolerance, accessed August 30, 2012. https://www.truetolerance.org/2012/key-facts-the-need-to-protect-parental-rights/.

[40] "Parental Involvement and Children's Academic Success," Familyfacts.org, The Heritage Foundation, accessed Feb. 8, 2012, http://www.thf_media.s3.amazonaws.com/familyfacts/briefs/FF_Brief_28.pdf.

[41] Resources to inform and equip: "IndoctriNation - Public Schools and the Decline of Christianity in America," http://www.indoctrinationmovie.com/; Albert R. Mohler, *Culture Shift: Engaging Current Issues with Timeless Truth* (Colorado Springs: Multnomah, 2008); Bruce N. Shortt, *The Harsh Truth about Public Schools* (Vallecito, CA: Chalcedon Foundation, 2004); Samuel L. Blumenfeld, *Is Public Education Necessary?* (Old Greenwich, CT: Devin-Adair, 1981).

CHAPTER 8: Threat #2: Redefine Value of Life

[1] "U.S. Abortion Statistics," Abort73.com, http://www.abort73.com/abortion_facts/us_abortion_statistics/.

[2] Randy Alcorn, "Scientists Attest to Life Beginning at Conception," http://www.naapc.org/why-life-begins-at-conception.

[3] "Facts on Induced Abortion in the United States," Sept. 15, 2012, http://www.guttmacher.org/pubs/fb_induced_abortion.html.

[4] Peter Singer, *Practical Ethics* (Cambridge: Cambridge UP, 1979), 85-86.

[5] Mayo Clinic staff, "Fetal Development: The First Trimester," Mayo Foundation for Medical Education and Research, last modified August 9, 2012, http://www.mayoclinic.com/health/prenatal-care/PR00112.

[6] Mark W. Foreman, *Christianity & Bioethics: Confronting Clinical Issues* (Joplin, MO: College Pub., 1999), 295.

[7] Steve Wagner, *Outline of the One-Minute Pro-life Apologist*, http://www.str.org/site/DocServer/One-Minute_Pro-Life_Apologist.pdf?docID=661.

[8] Go to www.numberofabortions.com and watch the number of abortions occurring every second of everyday.

[9] To watch Ray Comfort's 180video go to http://www.180movie.com/

[10] R.C. Sproul and Greg Bailey, *Abortion: A Rational Look at*

an Emotional Issue (Colorado Springs: NavPress, 1990), 150.

[11]   John Piper, *The Pleasures of God* (Portland: Multnomah, 1991), 263.

[12]   Stay alert and informed with these pro-life websites and initiatives: www.nrlc.org; www.lifenews.com; www. abort73.com.

CHAPTER 9: Threat #3: Replace Traditional Marriage

[1]   For more information read "Homosexuality and Child Sexual Abuse," http://www.frc.org/get.cfm?i=is02e3; and get educated on responding to homosexual advocacy in schools http://www.truetolerance.org/.

[2]   Tammy Bruce, *The Death of Right and Wrong: Exposing the Left's Assault on Our Culture and Values* (Roseville, CA: Forum, 2003), 89.

[3]   "About/History," GLSEN: Gay, Lesbian and Straight Education Network, accessed Sept. 9, 2012, http://www. glsen.org/cgi-bin/iowa/all/about/history/index.html.

[4]   For more information read MassResistance Special Report on *Template for Homosexual and Transgender Activism in Schools across the U.S.,* http://www.massresistance.org/docs/issues/kevin_jennings/1993_report/Jennings1993Report_Analysis.pdf.

[5]   "Change Your School," Gay-Straight Alliance Network." Accessed September 9, 2012, http://www. gsanetwork.org/get-involved/change-your-school.

[6]   David Kupelian, "Why Conservatives Are Abandoning

the Gay Issue," WND, published Aug. 16, 2010, http://
www.wnd.com/2010/08/192221/.

7   David A. Noebel, *Understanding the Times: The Collision
of Today's Competing Worldviews*, 2nd ed. revised (Manitou
Springs, CO: Summit Ministries, 2008), 142.

8   See Kinsey, A.C. W.B. Pomeroy, C.E. Martin (1948),
Sexual Behavior in the Human Male (Philadelphia: W.B.
Saunders) and Kinsey, A.C., W.B. Pomeroy, C.E. Martin,
P. H. Gebhard (1953), *Sexual Behavior in the Human Female*
(Philadelphia: W.B. Saunders).

9   "Answers to Your Questions for a Better Understanding
of Sexual Orientation & Homosexuality," American
Psychological Association, accessed Sept. 9, 2012, http://
www.apa.org/topics/sexuality/orientation.aspx.

10   Chris Gentilviso, "NAACP Endorses Gay Marriage
(UPDATE)," Huff Post Politics, updated May 20, 2012,
http://www.huffingtonpost.com/2012/05/19/naacp-gay-
marriage_n_1530029.html?ir=Black Voices.

11   Michael Brown, "Why Gay Is Not the New Black,"
Townhall.com, posted May 22, 2012, http://www.town-
hall.com/columnists/michaelbrown/2012/05/22/
why_gay_is_not_the_new_black/page/full/.

12   Noebel, *Understanding the Times*, 261.

13   "Responses to the Most Frequent Objections," National
Gay and Lesbian Task Force, Sept. 9, 2012, http://www.
thetaskforce.org/issues/parenting_and_family/questions.

14   Peter Sprigg, "The Top Ten Myths about

Homosexuality," http://www.downloads.frc.org/EF/ EF10F01.pdf.

[15] Stanton L. Jones and Mark A. Yarhouse, *Ex-gays? A Longitudinal Study of Religiously Mediated Change in Sexual Orientation* (Downers Grove, Ill.: IVP Academic, 2007), 124; summarizing findings of: J. Michael Bailey, Michael P. Dunne, and Nicholas G. Martin, "Genetic and environmental influences on sexual orientation and its correlates in an Australian twin sample," *Journal of Personality and Social Psychology,* Vol. 78(3), March 2000, 524-536.

[16] Norman L. Geisler, *Christian Ethics* (Grand Rapids: Baker, 1989), 266.

[17] Joseph Nicolosi, "New Study Confirms Homosexuality Can Be Overcome," NARTH, last updated May 1997, http://www.narth.com/docs/study.html.

[18] Greg Koukl, "Same-Sex Marriage Challenges and Responses," Stand to Reason, May-June 2004, http:// www.str.org/site/News2?page=NewsArticle&id=6553.

[19] Ibid.

[20] Noebel, *Understanding the Times,* 250.

[21] Tim Leslie, "The Case Against Same-Sex Marriage," LifeSiteNews.com, posted Feb. 23, 2004, http://www. lifesitenews.com/news/archive//ldn/2004/feb/040223a.

[22] Voddie Baucham, "Gay Is Not the New Black," The Gospel Coalition, posted July 19, 2012, http:// www.thegospelcoalition.org/blogs/tgc/2012/07/19/ gay-is-not-the-new-black/.

23 For example, see "Gay Marriage around the World," The Pew Forum on Religion and Public Life, http://www.pewforum.org/Gay-Marriage-and-Homosexuality/Gay-Marriage-Around-the-World.aspx.

24 Thomas E. Schmidt, *Straight & Narrow? Compassion & Clarity in the Homosexuality Debate* (Downers Grove, IL: InterVarsity, 1995), 108.

25 Alan P. Bell and Martin S. Weinberg, *Homosexualities: A Study of Diversity among Men and Women* (New York: Simon and Schuster, 1978), 308.

26 "Homosexuality Statistics," Conservapedia, accessed Sept. 9, 2012, http://www.conservapedia.com/Homosexuality_Statistics.

27 William Lane Craig, *Hard Questions, Real Answers* (Wheaton, IL: Crossway, 2003), 141-42.

28 "CDC Analysis Provides New Look at Disproportionate Impact of HIV and Syphilis among U.S. Gay and Bisexual Men," Centers for Disease Control and Prevention, posted Mar. 9, 2010, http://www.cdc.gov/nchhstp/Newsroom/msmpressrelease.html.

29 "Top 10 Things Lesbians Should Talk to Their Doctor About," About.com Lesbian Life, accessed Sept. 9, 2012, http://www.lesbianlife.about.com/od/lesbianhealth/tp/HealthConcerns.htm.

30 George Frater, *Our Humanist Heritage* (Maitland, FL: Xulon Press, 2010), 197.

31 For more information, read "The Health Risks of Gay

Sex" by John R. Diggs, M.D., http://www.catholiceduca-
tion.org/articles/homosexuality/healthrisksSSA.pdf.

[32] Kerby Anderson, "Gay Agenda in Schools," Probe
Ministries, http://www.probe.org/site/c.fdKEIMNsEoG/
b.4219121/k.48F3/Gay_Agenda_in_Schools.htm.

[33] "Homosexuality and Pederasty," Conservapedia,
accessed March 13, 2012, http://www.conservapedia.
com/Homosexuality_and_pederasty.

[34] Craig, *Hard Questions, Real Answers*, 141.

[35] Ibid.

[36] "Two Moms vs. Two Dads," *The Washington Times*,
published June 10, 2012, http://www.washingtontimes.
com/multimedia/image/gayjpg_734664/; Citizenlink
offers more detail of the study at http://www.citizenlink.
com/2012/06/11/study-children-of-parents-in-same-sex-
relationships-face-greater-risks/.

[37] "Study: Young Gay Men at Higher Risk of Suicide,"
365Gay.com, August 2, 2005; online at: http://
www.365gay.com/newscon05/08/080205suicide.htm
(page not available February 13, 2010; on file with author);
See, Sprigg, Peter, *Top Ten Myths about Homosexuality*.

[38] Lawrence Kurdek, "Are Gay and Lesbian Cohabiting
Couples *Really* Different from Heterosexual Married
Couples?" *Journal of Marriage and Family* 66, November
2004, 896.

[39] Peter Sprigg, *The Top Ten Harms of Same-Sex "Marriage"*; Lawrence Kurdek, "Are Gay and Lesbian Cohabiting Couples *Really* Different from Heterosexual Married Couples?" *Journal of Marriage and Family* 66.

[40] Leslie, "The Case Against Same-Sex Marriage."

[41] Support initiatives that fight against the agenda of GLSEN and agencies like them, www.nationformarriage.org; www.marriagedebate.com; www.afa.net.

[42] Get more information on how you can help homosexuals and preserve traditional marriage: *Exodus International, Family Research Council, Institute for Marriage and Public Policy, and Genesis Counseling.*

[43] Exodus International, Family Research Council, Institute for Marriage and Public Policy, and Genesis Counseling.

[44] Support the Defense of Marriage Act (DOMA) and U.S. state constitutional amendments banning same-sex marriages.

CHAPTER 10: Taking Back Our Family

[1] Timothy J. Keller and Kathy Keller, *The Meaning of Marriage: Facing the Complexities of Commitment with the Wisdom of God* (New York: Dutton, 2011), 48.

CHAPTER 11: God-Given Rights

[1] Matthew Spalding, *We Still Hold These Truths: Rediscovering Our Principles, Reclaiming Our Future* (Wilmington, DE: ISI, 2009), 35.

2   Ibid, 36.

3   Kevin Portteus, "An Apple of Gold: Abraham Lincoln and Constitutional Interpretation." Ashbrook Statesmanship Thesis, accessed July 25, 2012, http://www. ashbrook.org/wp-content/uploads/2012/06/2001-Portteus.pdf.

4 Spaulding, *We Still Hold These Truths*, 52.

5   Buckner F. Melton, *The Quotable Founding Fathers: A Treasury of 2,500 Wise and Witty Quotations from the Men and Women Who Created America* (Washington, DC: Brassey's, 2004), 224.

6   James Truslow Adams, *The Epic of America* (Boston: Little, Brown, 1935), 415.

CHAPTER 12: Threat #1: Remove the U.S. Constitution

1   Abraham Lincoln, "Abraham Lincoln Papers at the Library of Congress History," Library of Congress, accessed May 10, 2012, http://www.loc.gov/teachers/classroommaterials/connections/abraham-lincoln-papers/history3.html.

2   "Exhibit 1-8: The Media Elite Revisited," Media Research Center, Oct. 8, 2009, http://www.mrc.org/media-bias-101/exhibit-1-8-media-elite-revisited.

3   Norman L. Geisler and Frank Turek. *Legislating Morality: Is It Wise? Is It Legal? Is It Possible?* (Minneapolis: Bethany House, 1998), 57.

4   Williams J. Quirk and R. Randall Bridwell, *Judicial*

Dictatorship (New Brunswick: Transaction, 1995), 51.

⁵ Tobin Grant, "Conservatives Get 'Slap in the Face,'" *Christianity Today*, posted Aug. 6, 2010, http://www.christianitytoday.com/ct/2010/augustweb-only/41.51.0.html.

⁶ David Limbaugh, "The Judiciary's Culturally Sanctioned Allergy to Christianity Flourishes," Townhall. com, Aug. 20, 2010, http://townhall.com/columnists/davidlimbaugh/2010/08/20/the_judiciarys_culturally_sanctioned_allergy_to_christianity_flourishes.

⁷ Laura Ingraham, *Power to the People* (Washington, DC: Regnery, 2007), 108.

⁸ Ibid, 109.

⁹ "18. Judicial Review," Jefferson on Politics & Government: Judicial Review, accessed Sept.10, 2012. http://www.famguardian.org/Subjects/Politics/ThomasJefferson/jeff1030.htm.

¹⁰ Pat Robertson, *Courting Disaster: How the Supreme Court Is Usurping the Power of Congress and the People* (Nashville: Integrity, 2004), 73-74.

¹¹ See Edmund Burke, Paul Langford, and William B. Todd, *The Writings and Speeches of Edmund Burke* (Oxford: Clarendon, 1981).

¹² Mark R. Levin, *Liberty and Tyranny: A Conservative Manifesto* (New York: Threshold Editions, 2009), 37.

¹³ Ibid.

[14] "The Thomas Jefferson Papers at the Library of Congress History." Library of Congress, accessed Sept. 10, 2012. http://www.loc.gov/teachers/classroommaterials/connections/thomas-jefferson/history3.html.

CHAPTER 13: Threat #2: Redefine Government

[1] "Patrick Henry, Founders' Quotes," Founders' Quotes, Jan. 8, 2012, http://www.foundersquotes.com/quote-author/patrick-henry/.

[2] Noebel, *Understanding the Times*, 376.

[3] C.S. Lewis unravels the fragmented scheme of tyranny in his masterful work *The Humanitarian Theory of Punishment*. Lewis writes, "Of all tyrannies a tyranny sincerely exercised for the good of its victims may be the most oppressive. It may be better to live under robber barons than under omnipotent moral busybodies. The robber baron's cruelty may sometimes sleep, his cupidity may at some point be satiated; but those who torment us for our own good will torment us without end for they do so with the approval of their own conscience." Lewis, C. S., and Stuart Barton. Babbage. *C. S. Lewis on Punishment*. Appleford, Abingdon, Berks.: Marcham, 197, 6-7.

[4] John B. Taylor, *First Principles: Five Keys to Restoring America's Prosperity* (New York: Norton, 2012), 18.

[5] See Taylor, *First Principles*.

[6] See Frank York, "10 Reasons Why the EPA is a Clear and Present Danger," http://www.epaabuse.com/wp-content/uploads/2011/10/TenReasonsWhyTheEPAIsAClearAndPresentDanger.pdf.

[7] See Frank York, *10 Reasons Why the EPA is a Clear and Present Danger* (http://www.epaabuse.com/wp-content/uploads/2011/10/TenReasonsWhyTheEPAIsAClearAndPresentDanger.pdf).

[8] Rich Trzupek, *Regulators Gone Wild: How the EPA Is Ruining American Industry* (New York: Encounter, 2011) and Brian Sussman, *Eco-Tyranny: How the Left's Green Agenda Will Dismantle America* (Washington, DC: WND, 2012).

[9] "Reducing America's Energy Dependence," Natural Resources Defense Council, http://www.nrdc.org/air/transportation/gasprices.asp.

[10] Ali Ansari, *Confronting Iran* (New York: Basic, 2006), 2.

[11] See Mike Evans and Jerome R. Corsi, *Showdown with Nuclear Iran: Radical Islam's Messianic Mission to Destroy Israel and Cripple the United States* (Nashville: Nelson Current, 2006).

[12] Noebel, *Understanding the Times*, 358.

[13] Calvin E. Beisner, *Prosperity and Poverty: The Compassionate Use of Resources in a World of Scarcity* (Westchester, IL: Crossway, 1988), 34.

[14] Sunil Chaudhary, *Global Encyclopaedia of Welfare Economics* (New Delhi: Global Vision, 2009), 80.

[15] John Adams, Cutler and Russell, *Discourses on Davila: In a Series of Papers, on Political History, Written in the Year 1790, and Then Published in the Gazette of the United States* (Boston: Printed by Russell and Cutler, 1805).

[16]   James Robison and Jay Wesley Richards, *Indivisible: Restoring Faith, Family, and Freedom before It's Too Late* (NY: FaithWords, 2012), Ebook.

CHAPTER 14: Threat #3: Replace Freedoms

[1]   Samuel Adams, *The Writings of Samuel Adams,* Vol. II (New York: Putnam, 1906), 255.

[2]   See Patrick J. Buchanan, *State of Emergency: The Third World Invasion and Conquest of America* (New York: Thomas Dunne, 2006).

[3]   Buchanan, *State of Emergency,* 7.

[4]   Mike Huckabee, *A Simple Government: Twelve Things We Really Need from Washington (and a Trillion That We Don't!)* (New York: Sentinel, 2011), 132.

[5]   Steven Camarota, "Immigrants in the United States, 2007, A Profile of America's Foreign-Born Population." Center for Immigration Studies, Nov. 2007, http://www.cis.org/articles/2007/back1007.html.

[6]   P.F. Wagner, "Welcome To The Dark Side Of Illegal Immigration." The Dark Side of Illegal Immigration: Facts, Figures and Data Show a Disturbing Truth, Aug. 24, 2012, http://www.usillegalaliens.com/.

[7]   Michael Hugo Lopez and Michael Light, "A Rising Share: Hispanics and Federal Crime," http://www.pewhispanic.org/2009/02/18/a-rising-share-hispanics-and-federal-crime/.

[8]   Joseph Farah, "Illegal Aliens Murder 12 Americans

Daily," http://www.cis.org/articles/2007/back1007.html.

9   Deborah Schurman-Kauflin, "The Dark Side of Illegal Immigration: Nearly One Million Sex Crimes Committed by Illegal Immigrants in the United States," http://www.drdsk.com/articles.html#Illegals.

10   Jameson Taylor, "Illegal Immigration: Drugs, Gangs, & Crime," http://www.nccivitas.org/2007/illegal-immigration-drugs-gangs-and-crime/.

11   Patrick Radden Keefe, "Cocaine Incorporated," New York Times, http://www.nytimes.com/2012/06/17/magazine/how-a-mexican-drug-cartel-makes-its-billions.html?_r=3&pagewanted=1&ref=magazine.

12   "A Line in the Sand: Confronting the Threat at the Southwest Border," Majority Staff of the House Committee on Homeland Security, Subcommittee on Investigations, October 2006, 3.

13   Eric Ruark, and Jack Martin, "The Sinking Lifeboat: Uncontrolled Immigration and the U.S. Health Care System in 2009," Federation for American Immigration Reform, http://www.fairus.org/site/DocServer/health-care_09.pdf?docID=3521.

14   Karen Armstrong, "The True, Peaceful Face of Islam," Time, Sept. 23, 2001, http://www.time.com/time/magazine/article/0,9171,175987,00.html.

15   William J. Bennett, *Why We Fight: Moral Clarity and the War on Terrorism* (NY: Doubleday, 2002), 84.

16   See Erick Stakelbeck, *The Terrorist Next Door*

(Washington, DC: Regnery, 2011).

[17] This and all subsequent quotes from the Qur'an obtained from http://quran.com/. Hadith quotes obtained from http://hadithcollection.com/.

[18] See David P. Gaubatz, and Paul Sperry, *Muslim Mafia: Inside the Secret Underworld That's Conspiring to Islamize America* (Los Angeles: WND, 2009).

[19] See Andrew C. McCarthy, *The Grand Jihad: How Islam and the Left Sabotage America* (New York: Encounter, 2010).

[20] See Anois Shorrosh, *Islam Revealed: A Christian Arab's View of Islam* (Nashville: Thomas Nelson, 1988).

[21] See Joel C. Rosenberg, "Making Way for the Mahdi," Chap. 12, *Inside the Revolution* (Carol Stream, IL: Tyndale House, 2009).

[22] David Rubin, *The Islamic Tsunami: Israel and America in the Age of Obama.* (Israel: Shiloh Israel, 2010), 89.

[23] Brad Miner, *Smear Tactics: The Liberal Campaign to Defame America* (New York: HarperCollins, 2007), 275.

CHAPTER 15: Taking Back Our Country

[1] See Joel c. Rosenberg, *Implosion: Can America Recover from Its Economic and Spiritual Challenges in Time?* (Carol Stream, IL: Tyndale House, 2012).

[2] See Ronald Reagan and Douglas Brinkley, *The Reagan Diaries* (New York: HarperCollins, 2007).

³ Helpful U.S. Constitution resources: Hillsdale College Constitution Course; American Family Association, *Making the Constitution Obsolete DVD*; *The American Heritage Collection*; www.wallbuilders.com.

⁴ There are great financial programs that equip families to be a good steward of their money (e.g., Crown Financial and Financial Peace University).

⁵ America needs to end power grabs and closed-door deals of fraudulent handouts and entitlements that stifle growth; simplify the banking industry by monitoring big banks from corrupt broker-dealer deeds and secure opportunities for smaller banks; end NAFTA (North American Free Trade Agreement) so we can stop exporting more jobs and importing more consumer product at no cost to other countries; renegotiate terms and submit an amendment for withdraw from the World Trade Organization so they can no longer usurp the U.S. Constitution and steal American jobs. This will allow us better investment in future global trades with other countries to create more jobs in America and revitalize our economy.

⁶ With an unrelenting resolve to advance alternative energy, America can become (1) less dependent on foreign oil and more dependent on domestic oil; (2) productive in lowering emissions and pollutants; (3) strategic in reducing regulatory waste; (4) intentional on conserving energy and cleaning up the environment; (5) accelerate off-shore drilling with the proper oversight; (6) suspend massive tax hikes; (7) pay down our national debt by creating energy efficient jobs; (8) decrease national security threats by giving less money for oil to our enemies in Arab nations; (9) remain operative and functional in oil reserves to avoid global demand and risk our superpower status; (10) lower gas prices at the pump;

(11) reduce household electric bills; and (12) equalize shipment and food costs.

7 See *Christians at the Border: Immigration, the Church, and the Bible* (Grand Rapids: Baker Academic, 2008).

8 See Phil Valentine, "Illegal Immigration Is Dangerous to This Country," *The Conservative's Handbook: Defining the Right Position on Issues from A to Z.* (Nashville: Cumberland House, 2008).

9 For more information on the Islamic Revolution: *Answering Islam: A Christian-Muslim Dialogue*, answeringislam.org; *The Ministry of Joel Richardson*, joeltrumpet.com; *David Horowitz Freedom Center,* horowitzfreedomcenter. com; *Joel C. Rosenberg*, joelrosenberg.com; *Robert Spencer*, jihadwatch.org; *Clarion Fund*, radicalislam.com; *Center for Security Policy*, centerforsecuritypolicy.org; *Family Security Matters,* familysecuritymatters.org.

10 Edmund Burke, Paul Langford, and William B. Todd, *The Writings and Speeches of Edmund Burke* (Oxford: Clarendon, 1981).

Index

Abortion, 56, 71, 77-86
ACLU, 66, 167
Adams, Samuel, 159
Afghanistan, 166, 174
Allah, 168-171, 174, 176, 186
Amendments
    First, 33-34, 39-40, 98, 102, 133, 179
    Fifth, 81
    Tenth, 67
    Fourteenth, 39, 81, 102
America, 17-21, 31-48, 51-53, 128-130, 131-141, 143, 151,
    159-166, 171-176, 177-186
American
    Dream, 129-130, 143
    Revolution, 129
Apologetics, 46, 48
Arab Spring, 166, 176
Atheism, 65, 70

Baxter, Richard, 52
Bible
    Standards, 21-25, 31, 42, 46-47, 51-52, 58, 62, 66, 71,
    74, 79, 112, 113, 115-121, 128,   136, 137, 139, 151, 153-
    154, 175, 180, 184, 186-187, 192
Bill of Rights, 35, 107, 127, 156, 178
Blackstone, William, 126
Borders, 160-175, 183-185
Bureaucracy, 146, 148, 151, 153
Burke, Edmund, 140, 186
Butler Act, 66